7 REASONS
WHY YOU CAN
TRUST THE BIBLE

7REASONS
WHY YOU CAN
TRUST THE BIBLE

ERWIN W. LUTZER

MOODY PUBLISHERS
CHICAGO

All Scripture quotations, unless otherwise indicated, are taken from the New American
Standard Bible®, Copyright ©1960, 1962, 1963, 1968, 1971, 1972, 1973, 1975, 1977, 1995
by The Lockman Foundation. Used by permission. (www.Lockman.org)

Scripture quotations marked RSV are from the Revised Standard Version of the Bible, copyright 1952 [2nd edition, 1971] by the Division of Christian Education of the National
Council of the Churches of Christ in the USA. Used by permission. All rights reserved.

Scripture quotations marked NIV are taken from the Holy Bible, New International Ver-
sion®, NIV®. Copyright © 1973, 1978, 1984, 2011 by Biblica, Inc.™ Used by permission
of Zondervan. All rights reserved worldwide. www.zondervan.com. The "NIV" and "New
International Version" are trademarks registered in the United States Patent and Trademark
Office by Biblica, Inc.™

Scripture quotations marked ESV are taken from The Holy Bible, English Standard Version.
Copyright © 2000; 2001 by Crossway Bibles, a division of Good News Publishers. Used by
permission. All rights reserved.

Scripture quotations marked NKJV are taken from the New King James Version. Copyright
© 1982 by Thomas Nelson, Inc. Used by permission. All rights reserved.

Scripture quotations marked KJV are taken from the King James Version.

Cover design: Smartt Guys design and Erik M. Peterson
Interior design: Erik M. Peterson and Smartt Guys design
Cover photo: of magnifying glass on Bible copyright © by Pearl/Lightstock/60994. All
rights reserved.

Library of Congress Cataloging-in-Publication Data

Lutzer, Erwin W.
  Seven reasons why you can trust the Bible / Erwin W. Lutzer.
     p. cm.
  Includes bibliographical references.
  ISBN 978-0-8024-1331-4
  1. Bible—Evidences, authority, etc. I. Title.
  BS480.L78 2008
  220.1—dc22
                        2008024667

We hope you enjoy this book from Moody Publishers. Our goal is to provide high-quality,
thought-provoking books and products that connect truth to your real needs and challenges. For more information on other books and products written and produced from a
biblical perspective, go to www.moodypublishers.com or write to:

Moody Publishers
820 N. LaSalle Boulevard
Chicago, IL 60610

5 7 9 10 8 6

Printed in the United States of America

To Lynn and Shay Roush
May your trust in God's Word
guide your lives
in making disciples for Christ

"I shall delight in Your statutes;
I shall not forget Your word."
Psalm 119:16

CONTENTS

PREFACE

The prediction was both startling and accurate. T. H. Huxley, the biologist friend of Darwin, wrote in 1890 that he visualized the day when faith would be separated from fact and then faith would go on triumphantly forever. Of course, he and his friends must have considered such faith a joke, since it then would be up to each individual to choose whatever "faith" was right for him or her. As long as no one asked whether a belief was true, there could be as many different "faiths" as there are people in the world!

Huxley's day is here.

Listen to the talk shows, poke around the Internet, and

get caught up in the bestselling books on religion and philosophy, and you will be struck by the startling realization that the spirituality of our day has been divorced from facts. One can believe whatever one likes, no matter how contradictory or absurd. Every point of view, since it arises from one's own feelings, is just as valid as another. Faith is indeed "going on triumphantly forever."

Back in the nineteenth century, Alexis de Tocqueville, a French commentator, came to America and even then observed that for some Americans the goal was "to seek by themselves and in themselves for the only reason for things. . . . *So each man is narrowly shut up in himself, and from that basis makes the pretension to judge the world."* If that was true in the nineteenth century, how much more today. Thus whatever a person feels is the truth becomes the truth for him or her.

Obviously, dark days lie ahead for the believing church since Christianity is no longer providing the consensus for our society. The freedoms Christianity brought to us are being destroyed before our eyes. We are living at a time when humanistic thinking is coming to its natural conclusions in morals, education, and law. If we are to withstand the onslaught, we must be convinced in our own minds that we have a message from God, a sure word that "shines in a dark place." As Francis Schaeffer told us, only a strong view of Scripture can withstand the powerful pressure of relativistic thinking.

Schaeffer talked about a split in our modern culture variously described as between public/private or facts/values or secular/sacred. Secularists would like everyone to think the public or facts side represents scientific knowledge and objective facts, while the values side is just personal preferences and subjective choices.

Nancy Pearcey, in her book on competing worldviews, calls this division "the single most potent weapon for delegitimizing the biblical perspective in the public square today." She explains that secularists put religion into the "values" category, taking it out of the realm of true and false altogether: "Secularists can then assure us that of course they 'respect' religion, while at the same time denying that it has any relevance to the public realm."[1]

"To recover a place at the table of public debate, then, Christians must find a way to overcome the dichotomy between public and private, fact and value, secular and sacred. We need to liberate the gospel from its cultural captivity, restoring it to the status of public truth," she says.[2]

Many of us were born into a culture where the Bible was at least respected, if not believed and practiced. Even those who didn't accept the Bible acknowledged that whether the Bible was the Word of God mattered, because truth mattered. Truth, it was believed, was not something that arises within us, but rather something that has to be discovered by rational debate and evidence.

Today, all of this is lost. Our postmodern culture rejects the concept of absolute truth and instead embraces personal experience. Almost no one asks whether a belief is true; the question is whether it is "meaningful to me." Thus, we have a blizzard of conflicting claims, and millions of people have no desire to sort the true from the false, facts from fiction. We have gone from the belief that everyone has a right to his or her own opinion, to the absurd notion that every opinion is equally "right." Spirituality is a private matter; beliefs are accepted or rejected to suit one's fancy.

When the Bible, which is rooted in the soil of history and logic, is either rejected or reinterpreted to fit any belief, everyone is on their own to guess at the answer for ultimate questions. Since there is no umpire to judge various belief systems, the game of life is played with every participant creating his or her own rules. As a result, the Christian church is floundering, looking for an answer to today's spiritual and moral malaise. When we tell people we must return to the Bible, we often are pitied, looked upon as sincere but naive souls whom time has passed by.

Atheism, though representing only a small minority, has been gaining a high profile through the bestselling books and media appearances of its own high priests—who dismiss the Bible as a source of revelation and truth and insist that God does not exist. Their influence on our culture reveals the need for biblical understanding and truth.

"Although nonbelievers getting the upper hand isn't unprecedented in American culture, you have to go back 40 years to find a time when the country grappled with such a crisis of faith, an era marked by *Time* magazine's 1966 cover story 'Is God Dead?'" according to *Publishers Weekly.*[3]

This book is written with the deep conviction that the real battle of our day is not moral; it is not the proliferation of pornography, the desecration of our educational system, nor abortion on demand. All of these are but symptoms of failing to address the deeper question: *Has God left us a trustworthy revelation that tells us how to be reconciled to Himself?* Is truth something that I have a right to make up according to my liking, or is there an objective standard of rightness? Are there some religious convictions that are actually based on facts, beliefs that actually reflect the way things are? In other words, are there revealed truths that are based on *God?*

This book expounds seven reasons why I believe we can trust the Bible. If the Bible is based on facts, we have hope for our present crisis in religion and morality. If not, we must ruefully accept the despair of modern man who believes that no universal truths exist. We are then left with our own hunches, inclinations, and private interpretations of our own meaninglessness. Woody Allen speaks for many in this post-Christian era: "More than at any other time in history, mankind faces a crossroads. One path leads to despair and utter hopelessness; the other, to total extinction. Let us pray that we shall have the wisdom to choose correctly. I speak, by the way, not with any sense of futility, but with a panicky conviction of the absolute meaninglessness of existence."[4]

If there is any good news it will have to come from Christians who know what they believe and why. We are called to bring a message of hope in the midst of despair; we are asked to suffer if need be for the only message that shines a light in the darkness. Without a strong belief in the Scriptures, we simply will not be able to stand against the encroaching darkness. Francis Schaeffer told us many years ago: "Here is the great evangelical disaster—the failure of the evangelical world to stand for truth as truth. There is only one word for this—namely accommodation; the evangelical church has accommodated to the world spirit of the age."[5]

Schaeffer recognized, decades ago, that the Scriptures would be "the crucial area of discussion for evangelicalism in the next years." He was concerned about (1) liberal theologians who maintained that only the parts of the Bible not open to empirical research were actual revelation, and (2) scientists who were Christians who maintained the Bible is not authoritative in scientific matters. "We are left with the Bible as an authority only in religious matters," he wrote.[6] And that is exactly the argument many secularists are making today.

This book is also part of a personal journey. For more than thirty-five years, I have taught the Bible, preached the Bible, and tried, however imperfectly, to live by the Bible. In my youth I memorized several books of the New Testament, convinced that these were the very words of God. With the widespread neglect and even rejection of the Bible in today's culture, my own commitment to the Scriptures needed to be reconfirmed. I emerged from this study more confident than ever that God has spoken to us. He has not stuttered. We have a word from outside the universe, a love letter from a personal God.

I invite you to join me on my journey. Let us go back to the basics, back to the most fundamental question any human being could ask: *Has God spoken?* Are there credible reasons to believe that we can hold His revelation in our hands?

Is there a faith that is tied to facts?

Let's explore the evidence.

WAITING TO HEAR GOD SPEAK

S *peak to me!"*
Swedish film director Ingmar Bergman whispered these words while standing next to a portrait of Christ in a cathedral in Europe. He waited, but encountered only dead silence.

That experience, I'm told, was the motivation for Bergman's movie *Silence*, which portrayed people who despaired in trying to find God. In our world, he concluded, we hear only ourselves. No voice comes to us from outside the universe; when we seek a word from God, we are confronted with dead calm.

Bergman's story reminds me of a friend who is adamantly

convinced that God has not spoken to us. He was irritated when I told him that Christ's opinion of heaven and hell is what really mattered. "Why should I accept what the Bible says?" he asked. "The *Bible* was written by men, and by the way, *who decided what books should be in it anyway?*"

I'm not discounting the intellectual problems the Bible might have posed for this young student, but I also knew that, for him, belief in the Bible would entail a major lifestyle adjustment. I got the impression that he not only didn't believe that the Bible was the Word of God, but that he *wanted* to not believe it.

Why should anyone accept the Bible as a book from God? Our culture offers a long menu of religious options and assures us that they differ only in minor matters. We are invited to stand before this smorgasbord and choose whatever is "right" for us. Just the idea that there might be one book from God that judges all other religious opinions is discounted as narrow-minded bigotry. Then there's the atheism option that's getting trumpeted of late. This naturalistic, materialistic worldview denies the existence of anything supernatural, especially God, and maligns its God-fearing opponents as deranged, deluded, and even evil. It wants to free the world from religion, all the while looking much like a religion itself. "The total dogmatic conviction of correctness which pervades some sections of Western atheism today . . . immediately aligns it with a religious fundamentalism that refuses to allow its ideas to be examined or challenged," according to one Oxford professor who transitioned from atheist to Christian.[1]

Case in point, Sam Harris wrote his book *Letter to a Christian Nation,* "to arm secularists in our society, who believe that religion should be kept out of public policy, against their opponents on the Christian Right."[2] Not exactly broad-minded tolerance.

Despite these cultural pressures, Christianity claims to be a special, revealed religion. This sets it apart from what we might call the naturalistic religions. Hinduism, Buddhism, and a host of so-called New Age options are based on the insights of gurus, prophets, and "enlightened" leaders who presumably had more insight than the rest of us. These teachings, based on inner musings and personal experiences, are largely dependent on the subjective feelings of the teacher. No wonder the religions of the world offer an array of conflicting claims!

Of course there are also non-Christian prophets who claim to have messages from God. Whether it be Mary Baker Eddy, the prophet Muhammad, or Joseph Smith, all said that God had spoken through them. Understandably, many people surveying the religious landscape are confused. Some have given up on their quest for truth and assume that there is no one right path, no objective body of religious knowledge.

We must remember that revelations from God must be tested for consistency, authenticity, and truth. If God has spoken, we should expect that such a message is capable of serious investigation. It must stand above competing claims. Surely, such a revelation should have nothing to fear from fair-minded scholars and honest doubters intent on examining the credibility of the message.

Christianity says that God revealed truths about Himself that the most enlightened prophet could never discover. It claims that God personally sent us letters—written in human languages to be sure—but nevertheless containing His words. The book called the Bible claims to lead us into the metaphysical realm (that which lies beyond our senses) where no unaided human mind has the ability to venture. Indeed, it purports to give us privileged information about God and His relationship to the world. Here, finally, we find some answers to the great mysteries of our existence. If the Bible is a message from God, then we can say, "If the Bible says it, God says it."

Even if the Bible contained only an absolute moral code, it would have to be a book from God. The philosopher Ludwig Wittgenstein did not believe in the Bible, but he knew that we as finite human beings cannot discover moral absolutes on our own. He said that if an objective ethical standard existed, it would have to come to us from a being independent of the universe. He wrote, "If a man could write a book on Ethics which really was a book on Ethics, this book would, with an explosion, destroy all the books in the world."[3] In this book I hope to show that the Bible is a reliable book on matters about God, man, salvation, eternity, and morality too. *With an explosion, it does destroy all other books in the world!*

Here are some questions the Bible answers: Do we exist after death? If yes, what can we expect on the other side? Can we be sure that we will spend eternity with God? Will the future be brighter than the past? How can we best interpret both the joys and sorrows of this present existence? Most important, does God love the world or should we interpret cruel natural disasters and human suffering as proof that in the end He is sadistic and indifferent to our plight?

Now, if God has *not* spoken, if we are on our own on this cosmic speck in a vast purposeless universe, then we must do the best we can with the cosmos as we find it. Let us not flinch from the frightful conclusions to which we must come. In a world where there is no existence beyond the grave and everything will ultimately be destroyed, we must agree with the atheist Bertrand Russell, that in such a world everything is meaningless. The scales of justice will never be balanced and our desire for significance will have to be squelched. As Woody Allen put it, "We have no spiritual center. We are adrift alone in the cosmos."

Atheists are now promising "a world of new hope and unlimited horizons—once we have shed this delusion of God. . . . The reality is the emptiness that results from the loss of the transcendent is stark and devastating, both philosophically and existentially. . . . One finds oneself in the vise-like grip of despair in a life without ultimate purpose," as Ravi Zacharias learned for himself. While a young atheist, Zacharias came to prefer the oblivion of death "to the sheer weight of the emptiness of a God-less world" until he encountered Jesus, who "spelled the difference between despair and hope" for him.[4]

Friedrich Nietzsche, who prepared Germany for Hitler by his belief in a superman, said, regarding God, "We have killed Him, but who will wipe the blood from our hands?" Yes, if God either does not exist or is fundamentally unknowable, there is no answer either for our guilt or for our deepest longings for significance.

But if God *has* spoken, we can probe His words, study His ways, and heed His commandments. The Bible, if it is true, is like a light shining in a musty basement, guiding us to the door that leads to eternal life.

THE PURPOSE OF THIS BOOK

The purpose of this book is to give reasons why I believe God has left us with a written revelation. In short, I shall present the reasonableness of the Christian conviction that the Bible is the Word of God. This evidence is open to investigation, it is "out there," and it invites discussion and argumentation.

If you are already a believer in the Bible, this book will validate your belief; if you are a fair-minded skeptic it will challenge your thinking about a book that has had an immeasurable impact on the history of the world. Take it or leave it, the Bible is not a book that can be ignored.

Can I "prove" that the Bible is the Word of God? The answer, as you might guess, depends on what is meant by "proof." No matter what evidence is presented, there must always be room for faith, a reasonable faith to be sure, but faith nonetheless. (Since the question of "proof" and "assurance" needs a fuller explanation, I discuss these matters in more detail in the "For Further Consideration" section in chapter 1.)

I have a friend who says he saw a beautiful house standing opposite Mont Blanc on the border between France and Switzerland. What puzzled him was that the shutters on the windows that faced the beautiful mountain were always closed. No matter how remarkable the Bible is, it will not have an appeal to those who refuse to give it an honest hearing. At the end of the day, whether we believe it depends on whether we are willing to fling the shutters open and see what is before us.

With the onslaught of the modern *zeitgeist* (spirit of the age) that chips away at the notion of biblical authority, I trust that this rigorous review and restatement of the trustworthiness of Scripture will stimulate discussion and inspire confidence. I pray that those of us who already love the Bible will love it more; and that those who have, for whatever reason, come to distrust it, will be led to the conviction that God has indeed given us a letter that can be believed. We can be thankful we are not alone in the cosmos.

I have chosen seven reasons why I believe we can trust the Bible; others might believe that there are many more arguments that can be examined. I have selected those that I believe are most relevant and accessible to the modern thinker. I attempt to answer questions such as:

- Isn't it illogical to say that the Bible is the Word of God just because it claims to be?
- Can we trust the history of the Bible?
- What about the miracles?
- Why are the Dead Sea Scrolls important?
- Can we believe the prophecies of the Bible?
- Could not the disciples have made up the stories about Christ?
- Doesn't science contradict the Bible?
- Who decided what books would be in the Bible and when was the decision made?
- What about the gospel of Thomas and other lost books?
- What does the Bible teach us that other books don't?
- What benefits come to those who study the Bible?

We'll try to answer these questions and more along the way. Perhaps you will be surprised at the reasons why we can be sure that the Bible is a unique book that originated in the mind of God. In contrast to all the other religions of the world, only Christianity has a book with purpose. Only a personal God can faithfully intervene in our lives.

I don't agree with everything Oliver Wendell Holmes wrote, but I like his assessment of truth. "Truth is tough. It will not break like a bubble at a touch; nay, you may kick it about all day like a football, and it will be round and full at evening."[5]

And so I invite you to come with me on a journey, to examine the Bible with a critical eye to see whether it has the marks of a supernatural revelation. Let us look at the evidence as it exists, willing to learn, ask, probe, and evaluate. I promise that the Bible will not break, and the truth will be around at the end of the day.

UNDERSTANDING
DUAL AUTHORSHIP

When theologians say that the Bible is the Word of God, what do they mean? Many people interpret this phrase to mean that God dictated the Bible to the authors who did little more than write word for word what they were told. Like a good secretary who has learned to transcribe dictation, the authors of the Bible, it is said, were passive vehicles while God told them what to write.

This is *not* what I mean when I say that the Bible is the Word of God. Even the casual reader notices that the authors of Scripture wrote with different styles, literary organization, and even grammar. These differences become even more apparent to those who read the Bible in the original languages of Hebrew, Aramaic, and Greek.

The apostle Paul wrote carefully reasoned treatises, often betraying his own disappointments, encouragements, or even anger. Mark, in his account of the life of Jesus, used the vivid present tense when he described Christ's walk throughout the land. His Greek was so rough that he even appears to have used odd grammar, no doubt reflecting his own speaking habits. Sometimes New Testament authors just paraphrased the Old Testament, not quoting it word for word. When they reported the number of people who died in a plague, they used round numbers, just as reporters do today.

We can identify at least three different kinds of inspiration. For example, some things the authors wrote they knew by *ordinary means*. Luke, for example, said that he did careful research before he wrote his account of the life of Christ, just as did others who were eyewitnesses of Jesus: "It seemed fitting for me as well," he wrote, "having investigated everything carefully from the beginning, to write it out for you in consecutive order, most excellent Theophilus; so that you may know the exact truth about the things you have been taught" (Luke 1:3–4). Perhaps he was not even aware that he was writing Holy Scripture when he wrote his account of Christ's life and ministry. He just recorded what he had investigated and what he had seen.

Second, in some instances God endowed the authors with *ideas that they were allowed to write in their own words.* This freedom allowed Paul, for example, not only to write with his own style, but also to transition from doctrinal to personal matters. In his second letter to Timothy he could speak with authority about God's knowledge of us in eternity past (2 Timothy 1:9) and yet later say, "When you come bring the cloak which I left at Troas with Carpus, and the books, especially the parchments" (2 Timothy 4:13). God's ideas were written in Paul's style and in line with his interests and abilities.

Then, also, some of the Bible was *dictated by God word for word.* Moses did not add his own style when he wrote, "You shall have no other gods before Me." On many occasions the prophets received revelations from God, word for word. At other times they put the message in their own words. But dictation, as such, was rare; almost always the author's style can be recognized.

A moment's reflection will tell us what has happened in the history of biblical scholarship. Naturalists who balk at the idea that God has supernaturally revealed Himself conclude that the Bible is a purely human book. It is, they say, a history of what men have thought about God. Miracles are discounted as exaggerations, or even mythology. These scholars emphasize that the Bible was written by men, and *only* by men. Sometimes brilliant, sometimes boring, sometimes accurate, and sometimes riddled with error, it was simply a history of what biblical writers believed was the revelation of God. For such scholars the human authorship of the Bible overshadows its divine origin.

More recently a rash of books and films by atheist zealots have mocked the Bible's authority and the existence of God Himself.

Sam Harris, atheist author, points out, correctly, "There are many books that pretend to divine authorship, and they make incompatible claims about how we all must live."[6] While not all of these conflicting accounts can be true, that does not mean that none of them can be true. Harris fails to show that he has looked deeply into whether the one true God and Creator of the universe has revealed Himself in the Bible, along with His will for how we must live.

Beyond denying God's written revelation, some atheists are very loudly and publicly proclaiming their denial of God's existence as well: "I am not attacking any particular version of God or gods. I am attacking God, all gods, anything and everything supernatural, wherever and whenever they have been or will be invented," says Oxford professor and evolutionary biologist Richard Dawkins.[7] His religion is materialistic naturalism—only observable matter exists, nothing else, and everything can be explained by natural causes.

One scientist goes so far as to claim in his book that science proves that God does not exist.[8]

He and some atheist scientists like him try to do that by using probabilities. It's the best they can do. That's because every worldview comes with assumptions. In the end, every religious worldview, including atheism, requires some faith. Norman Geisler and Frank Turek explain why in their book *I Don't Have Enough Faith to Be an Atheist:*

"As limited human beings, we do not possess the type of knowledge that will provide us with absolute proof of God's existence or nonexistence. Outside of the knowledge of our own existence ... we deal in the realm of probability." Using good evidence concerning the big questions about God and life and the truth of Scripture, one can conclude with, say, 95 percent certainty. That's the best fallible and finite humans can do, and it's sufficient for the biggest life decisions, they explain.[9]

Older fundamentalists and a few evangelicals have frequently swung to the opposite extreme. Some at least have been at pains to shun historical and critical studies of the Bible, fearing that the very process would eclipse its divine authorship. A few have actually held to the dictation theory of inspiration, teaching that the biblical authors acted as stenographers, passively recording God's message word for word. In their zeal to defend the Bible as the Word of God, these scholars have allowed the divine origin of the Bible to overshadow the human side.

We can avoid these extremes by admitting that the Bible is of *dual* authorship. It is a book of God *and* a book of man. God's part was to superintend the writing of the books, revealing His will. Man's part was to write this revelation using a human language and style so that God's message was preserved for future generations.

But "to err is human," we are told, and, since the Bible did not fall out of the sky but was written by fallible human beings, it must have its flaws. But such reasoning discounts God's omnipotence. If He wished to speak to us, it is easy to believe that He could superintend and inspire the writers to accurately record His revelation.

Although we are all fallible human beings, we all have written some infallible statements (for example, "Winston Churchill was at one time the prime minister of England"). In the case of the Scriptures, such accurate statements are made not only about history, but also about theology and even science. The point, of course, is that *fallible human beings can write an infallible message.*

The Bible has dual authorship, just as Christ has two natures. Christian theology maintains that Christ was fully God and fully human, the two natures united in one person. And just as Christ was fully human and yet sinless, just so the Bible is fully human and yet without error.

Again we can see that liberal theologians have emphasized Christ's humanity to the exclusion of His divinity. Just look at Him as He sits on the well, weary with His journey. See Him as He sleeps on the boat and when He cries, "I thirst." Surely, say the religious liberals, He was a remarkable man, but *only* a man nevertheless.

Interestingly, in the early centuries of the church, some went to the opposite extreme. They denied Christ's humanity and affirmed only His deity. They thought that if God were to become man, He would have had to accept imperfection. So they said Christ only *seemed* to be man; His divinity canceled His humanity.

Just as the humanity of Christ is a stumbling block to

many who then deny His deity, even so the humanity of the Bible is a stumbling block to those who deny its divine origin. But the Scriptures present Christ as *both* fully God and fully man. Yes, even when He was weary, perplexed, and in the throes of Gethsemane, He was God. And when He said, "Before Abraham was born, I am" (John 8:58), He was man. *Just so, both the divine and the human authorship of the Scriptures must be fully appreciated.*

Consider the similarities between the Christ (the incarnate Word) and the Bible (the written Word).

- Both are eternal.

    OF CHRIST: "In the beginning was the Word, and the Word was with God, and the Word was God" (John 1:1).

    OF THE SCRIPTURES: "Forever, O LORD, your word is firmly fixed in heaven" (Psalm 119:89 ESV).

- Both are conceived by the Holy Spirit.

    OF CHRIST: "The angel answered and said to her, 'The Holy Spirit will come upon you, and the power of the Most High will overshadow you; and for that reason the holy Child shall be called the Son of God'" (Luke 1:35).

    OF THE SCRIPTURES: "No prophecy was ever made by an act of human will, but men moved by the Holy Spirit spoke from God" (2 Peter 1:21).

- Both are human and yet without error.

    OF CHRIST: "For we do not have a high priest who cannot sympathize with our weaknesses, but One who has been tempted in all things as we are, yet without sin" (Hebrews 4:15).

    OF THE SCRIPTURES: "The Scripture cannot be broken" (John 10:35).

• Both have a unique authority.

OF CHRIST: "He taught them as one having authority, and not as the scribes" (Mark 1:22 NKJV).

OF THE SCRIPTURES: "Hear, O heavens, and give ear,
O earth; for the Lord has spoken" (Isaiah 1:2 RSV).

No wonder Christ is called "The Word of God"! When
He returns to earth, John describes Him: "He is clothed with
a robe dipped in blood, and His name is called The Word
of God" (Revelation 19:13). Just as it is difficult for us to
explain the divine mystery of the *incarnation,* even so it is
difficult for us to explain the mystery of divine *inspiration.*
In both instances God accommodated Himself to human
beings; in both instances He has given us a revelation that is
at once human and divine.

The following tribute to the Bible was written by an unknown poet:

> *Deep strike Thy roots, O heavenly vine*
> *Into our earthy sod*
> *Most human, yet most divine*
> *The flower of man and God*

In this book we shall not shield ourselves from the human characteristics of the Bible, nor shall we shrink from the
evidence for its divine origin. Let us boldly affirm that God
who became man is the same God who inspired common
men to write a very uncommon book.

THE CHALLENGE OF DEFINITION

I believe that the Bible, as it was written in the original manuscripts, is the *infallible* and *inspired* Word of God. What

does this mean? And what does it *not* mean?

First, we mean much more than that the Bible is free from error. It might be possible for a historian to write a history of Rome that is accurate, yet the author claims no special inspiration from God. Thus, the Bible is not only accurate, but also the "breath of God," coming to us endued with a power that is not the property of other books. In short, the Bible carries the *authority* of God.

Second, we mean much more than simply that the Bible is an inspiring book. We have all read novels or poetry that have inspired us. Through these means we have been given moments of insight, emotional energy, and a vista of new ideas. But when we speak of the *inspiration* of the Bible, we mean something else.

Parts of the Bible might not inspire us at all; indeed, there are whole chapters that might appear irrelevant and dull. This does not diminish the fact that the Bible is the Word of God. The question is not whether the message is exciting, whether we feel good about it, or even whether it changes our lives. The question is, Is the message presented *true?* Does it come with God's signature?

Third, it means more than simply saying that the Bible is inspired in matters of doctrine, but not in matters of science and history. Some scholars have insisted that the Bible is inspired when pointing toward Christ, but may contain contradictions and errors in matters of lesser importance.

Such reasoning is wrongheaded. As we shall point out later in more detail, the historical and the doctrinal matters are interwoven and can't be separated. Is the resurrection of Christ a historical event? Or is it a matter of doctrine too? Obviously, it is both. What is more, if we cannot trust the Bible in matters of history, why should we trust it in matters of doctrine? In fact, we shall argue that the reliability of the Bible in earthly matters gives us confidence to believe the Bible in heavenly matters.

Fourth, we must understand that the very words of Scripture are important. We cannot say, as some have, that the ideas are inspired but the words are not. Linguistic analysis has demonstrated that every genuine word carries a genuine meaning; a wrong word, therefore, carries a wrong meaning. No wonder Christ said, "For truly I say to you, until heaven and earth pass away, not the smallest letter or stroke shall pass from the Law until all is accomplished" (Matthew 5:18).

Often the writers of Scripture were free to choose their own words, as long as the meaning of those words was within the bounds of truth. This explains why different words might be used to explain the same event. Matthew, when describing the reaction of the disciples to Christ's walking on the water, used the word *proskuneo,* meaning "to worship" (14:33). Mark, recording the same event, used the word *existēmi,* which means "to be amazed" (Mark 6:51). Each word gives a different meaning, but both are accurate.

Obviously, since tape recorders were not available, the writers often recorded the gist of a conversation without pretending to write it down word for word. Inerrancy (that the Bible is without error) means only that there was a faithful representation of the content, not that the speeches were recorded verbatim or in full.

We must also keep in mind that a report can be imprecise and yet true. Wayne Grudem of Phoenix Seminary gives the example, "My home is not far from my office" as a statement that is completely true, but imprecise. In the Bible, we sometimes find round numbers or approximations in measurements and battle figures.

Also, the authors of the Bible employed the language of description when speaking about scientific matters. We cannot say the writers of Scripture erred because they spoke of a sunrise, even though Copernicus taught us that what we call a sunrise is actually the earth rotating toward the sun. The authors of the Bible used the same descriptive language as a modern almanac. By speaking of the sunrise, the Bible does not teach that the sun goes around the earth.

Finally, we must keep in mind that *infallibility* (freedom from error) is applied only to the original manuscripts, the parchments upon which the Old and New Testament authors wrote their messages. What we have today are copies of copies, and hence it is possible that errors in transmission have crept into the text.

Of what value is the doctrine of inerrancy if the original manuscripts no longer exist? The answer is not difficult to grasp. *It is the inerrancy of the originals that makes the reconstruction of the original text so important.* Thanks to careful scribes in centuries past and thoughtful scholars today, we can have before us a text that, for all practical purposes, reflects the original manuscripts. *We can say with confidence that the Bible we hold in our hands is "The Word of God."*

Think of it this way. Suppose a schoolteacher were to receive a letter personally written and signed by the president of the United States. She is excited to share the letter with her pupils so asks them to record it in their notebooks, word for word. Then, let us suppose the letter is lost and she must use her student notebooks to reconstruct the contents. She discovers that one student has two misspelled words, another misunderstood a phrase, and yet another missed the last word of a sentence. Yet with the notebooks in front of her, would anyone deny that she has the resources to essentially reconstruct the contents of the president's letter? Precisely because each word of the letter came from the president, the attempt to get all of the words accurate is a very important task.

If you have ever looked at a Hebrew Old Testament or the Greek New Testament, you will see numerous footnotes indicating variations in the text (many of these are found in the margins of English Bibles too). Please keep in mind that the manuscripts of the Bible have been carefully copied, and from these copies other copies have been made. Some were copies made in the same language; others were translations. Today, centuries later, we have thousands of copies of various ages and degrees of accuracy. Obviously, there are bound to be innumerable variations among these later manuscripts. Most of them have to do with spelling and word order.

But the good news is that each variation can be evaluated, based on careful scholarship and painstaking comparisons. Virtually no variations would affect doctrinal matters. No credible scholar would dispute the fact that the content of the Bible we have in our hands is essentially that found in the original manuscripts.

Thanks to archaeology, the discovery of ancient manuscripts (like the Dead Sea Scrolls), and the study of textual criticism, we can be more confident than our forefathers that we do indeed have, for all practical purposes, the contents of those original texts. With all due allowance for human error in copying, we can rejoice that we have the undiluted message of God in our hands.

A PROMISE FOR YOU

"If I were the devil," wrote J. I. Packer, "one of my first aims would be to stop folk from digging into the Bible.... I should do all I could to surround it with the spiritual equivalent of pits, thorns, hedges, and man traps to frighten people off."[10] Thanks be, the devil cannot keep us from probing the depths of Scripture.

Certainly, secular attacks on the Bible's credibility have stepped up lately: "Ever since the nineteenth century, scholarly theologians have made an overwhelming case that the gospels are not reliable accounts of what happened in the history of the real world," says Dawkins. "All were written long after the death of Jesus, and also after the epistles of Paul, which mention almost none of the alleged facts of Jesus' life. . . . All were then copied and recopied . . . by fallible scribes who, in any case, had their own religious agendas."[11]

Here, Dawkins attempts to make liberal theologians representative of biblical scholarship in general and just ignores the large body of conservative scholars who would disagree.

The late systematic theology professor Bernard Ramm noted the meticulous care that scribes took in transcribing copies of the Scriptures by hand: "In reference to the Old Testament we know that the Jews preserved it as no other manuscript has ever been preserved. . . . They kept tabs on every letter, syllable, word, and paragraph. They had special classes of men within their culture whose sole duty was to preserve and transmit these documents with practically perfect fidelity—scribes, lawyers, massoretes. Who ever counted the letters and syllables and words of Plato or Aristotle? Cicero or Seneca?"[12]

Through textual criticism, scholars have studied and compared a great many ancient Bible (and other) manuscripts with the goal of reconstructing the original version as closely as possible.

Author Josh McDowell writes: "Compared with other ancient writings, the Bible has more manuscript evidence to support it than any ten pieces of classical literature combined. . . . There are more than 5,686 known Greek manuscripts of the New Testament. Add over 10,000 Latin Vulgate and at least 9,300 other early versions, and we have close to, if not more than, 25,000 manuscript copies of portions of the New Testament in existence today. No other document of antiquity even begins to approach such numbers."[13]

"We are informed by no less an authority than Kenyon [F. G. Kenyon, *Handbook to the Textual Criticism of the New Testament*, 2nd ed. (Grand Rapids: Eerdmans, 1951), 3–5] that of the plays of Aeschylus there are 50 copies; of the works of Sophocles, 100 copies; of the Greek anthology, 1 copy; and of Catallus, 3 independent manuscripts. The earliest manuscript of Sophocles is 1400 years after his death; and the same holds for Aeschylus, Aristophanes, and Thucydides. For Euripedes it is 1600 years, 1300 for Plato, 1200 for Demonsthenes, 900 for Horace, 700 for Terrence, 500 for Livy, 1000 for Lucretius, and 1600 for Catallus. The New Testament has an attestation of [thousands of] Greek manuscripts, coming from the second (John Rylands fragment of John, P56) and third century (Chester Beatty Papyri) and fourth century (Codices Vaticanus and Sinaiticus)," writes Professor Ramm.[14]

In fact, one Dallas Seminary professor, Daniel Wallace, has been progressing on his goal to photograph 1.3 million pages of New Testament manuscripts known to exist, so as to preserve them for future study. Some of those nearly complete manuscripts exist from roughly 300 years after Jesus' birth.[15]

The Scriptures themselves give us this promise. "Blessed is the man . . . [whose] delight is in the law of the Lord, and in His law he meditates day and night. He will be like a tree firmly planted by streams of water, which yields its fruit in its season, and its leaf does not wither; and in whatever he does, he prospers" (Psalm 1:1–3). The following quote from Robert Chapman is long, but it deserves a careful reading.

> This book contains the mind of God, the state of man, the way of salvation, the doom of sinners, and the happiness of believers. Its doctrines are holy, its precepts binding, its histories are true and its decisions are immutable. Read it to be wise, believe it to be safe, and practice it to be holy. It contains light to direct you, food to support you, and comfort to cheer you. It is the traveler's map, the pilgrim's staff, the pilot's compass, the soldier's sword, and the Christian's charter. Here paradise is restored, heaven opened, and the gates of hell disclosed. Christ is its grand subject, our good its design, and the glory of God its end. It should fill the memory, test the heart, and guide the feet.
>
> Read it slowly, frequently, prayerfully. It is a mine of wealth, a paradise of glory and a river of pleasure. It is given you in life, it will be opened at the judgment, and be remembered forever. It involves the highest responsibility, rewards the greatest labor and condemns all who will trifle with its sacred contents.[16]

The Bible is a book of answers, not a book of questions. It guides us in matters where the mind cannot penetrate, and where human reason leaves us unsatisfied. Many blessings are given to those who begin an honest search, willing to follow the trail of truth wherever it might lead.

The famous preacher George Whitefield said, "God has condescended to become an author, and yet people will not read His writings. There are very few that ever gave this Book of God, the grand charter of salvation, one fair reading through." The love letter is before us, waiting to be read. We owe it to ourselves to give this book "a fair reading through."

Voltaire said that in a generation the Bible would be outdated, but after his death, his house was purchased by the Geneva Bible Society to spread Bibles throughout Europe. As we shall see, the Bible has often been pronounced dead, but the corpse never stays put.

In France there is a monument to the Huguenots who died as martyrs for the cause of Christ. Acknowledging that the Bible has been able to withstand the hammer blows of its critics, these words are inscribed on the monument:

> *Hammer away, ye unregenerate hands*
> *Your hammer breaks, God's anvil stands.*

The Bible is strong enough to withstand the blows of its severest critics; it is able to assuage our doubts and inspire confidence that God has spoken. Join me on a journey that will investigate the most remarkable book in the world.

Bring your questions, bring your doubts, and don't forget your heart.

ONE: A LOGICAL REASON

THE BIBLE CLAIMS TO BE GOD'S WORD

The Bible is the Word of God because it *claims* to be the Word of God!"

"That," said my philosophy professor, "is a perfect example of circular reasoning. Christians simply assume the point they wish to prove!"

Yes, there it was. My professor had found a column in a newspaper written by a prominent Christian who argued that the Bible was the Word of God because its authors claimed to be divinely inspired. The professor then took a moment to insist that this was equivalent to saying, "I'm telling the truth because I'm telling you that I'm telling the truth!" The implication was clear: the better we are able to think, the less likely we will be Christians!

Was my professor justified in his criticism? Of course, the bare statement "The Bible is the Word of God because it claims to be" is logically suspect. We all know how naive it is to be asked why we believed a stranger and then reply, "I know he was telling the truth because he told me he was!" We've all met people who expect us to accept their word without independent confirmation.

That said, let us not be too hasty in dismissing what the Bible has to say about itself. Let us suppose a foreigner would arrive on our shores and we would like to know something about his background, nationality, and history. We might call on a number of experts to investigate his clothing, others to study his facial features, and a third group knowledgeable about the history of rafting to make an informed guess regarding the age and origin of this man's mode of transportation.

Assuming our guest could speak our language, would it be illogical to interview him? Certainly we would want to test what he had to say, checking for consistency, but should we not presume he is telling the truth unless there are reasons to believe otherwise?

In fact, there are some truths about people that we might never know unless they were to tell us. Years of independent study and analysis might never yield the kind of details that an individual might share in a few moments of conversation. Common courtesy means that we give a person a chance to tell his or her story. Just so, we must have enough respect for the Bible to "hear it out," as the saying goes.

In a court of law the defendant is allowed to speak for himself. He is permitted to defend his integrity, to give reasons why his version of events is correct. He should have more to say than simply, "I am innocent." He must be given the opportunity to show that his report is consistent, worthy of belief. Cross-examination should either confirm or deny his version of the story.

Just as a defendant might be telling the truth about himself, so the Bible might be telling the truth about itself. In the end you might choose to reject what it has to say about its origin, but if so, I hope you have the courage to face the implications. If you board the train of unbelief, you will have to take it all the way to its destination. More on that later.

Of course, we will also bring other witnesses to the courtroom. In subsequent chapters we will call history, prophecy, science, and Christ Himself to the witness stand. But we have every right to give the Bible a fair hearing and, as best we can, put it through a cross-examination.

We do not have to search for long to find what the Bible has to say about itself; the claims of divine origin are found on nearly every page. Let's examine a few. Then we will analyze what this means for you and me.

IN THE BIBLE'S OWN WORDS

Perhaps you think, "Of course the Bible declares itself to be inspired by God; why even bother presenting the evidence?" But there are reasons why we must review these claims and their implications. Stay with me as we take a quick tour of some fascinating biblical terrain.

"All Scripture is breathed out by God and profitable for teaching, for reproof, for correction, and for training in righteousness, that the man of God may be complete, equipped for every good work" (2 Timothy 3:16–17 ESV). This is one of the clearest and best-known statements in the Scriptures about the origin of the Scriptures. The English word *inspiration*, with its prefix *in*, gives the impression that after the various books of the Bible were written, God breathed into them, so that they were "inspired." But the Greek word means that God *"breathed* out" and the result was the Scriptures. In other words, *the Bible, metaphorically speaking, is the breath of God.*

In the Old Testament the "mouth of God" was regarded as the source from which the divine message came. "By the word of the Lord the heavens were made, and by the breath of His mouth all their host" (Psalm 33:6). That expression, "breath of His mouth," is the Hebrew equivalent of "God breathed." God, the Creator, used men to write the Scriptures, but they are God speaking. The same mouth that spoke all of creation into existence is the mouth that spoke producing the Scriptures.

Inspiration does not just mean that God approved of their writings, but that men actually wrote His words. His ideas became their ideas, and they accurately recorded what He wanted us to know. Let us survey the Old and New Testaments to see if this is a fair statement of what the Bible claims.

THE CLAIMS OF
THE OLD TESTAMENT

Let's reread, as if for the first time, a few of the claims that the writers of the Old Testament have made. Look for the phrase "The Lord said" or its equivalent.

- "Then God spoke all these words, saying, 'I am the Lord your God, who brought you out of the land of Egypt, out of the house of slavery. You shall have no other gods before Me. You shall not make for yourself an idol'" (Exodus 20:1–4).

- "Then the Lord said to Moses, 'See, I make you as God to Pharaoh, and your brother Aaron shall be your prophet. You shall speak all that I command you, and your brother Aaron shall speak to Pharaoh that he let the sons of Israel go out of his land'" (Exodus 7:1–2).

- "He humbled you and let you be hungry, and fed you with manna which you did not know, nor did your fathers know, that He might make you understand that man does not live by bread alone, but man lives by everything that proceeds out of the mouth of the Lord" (Deuteronomy 8:3).

- "Listen, O heavens, and hear, O earth; for the Lord speaks" (Isaiah 1:2).

- "The words of Jeremiah ... to whom the word of the Lord came" (Jeremiah 1:1–2). Five more times in the first chapter of Jeremiah we read that the word of the Lord came to this prophet (vv. 4, 9, 11, 13).

Of course there are hundreds of instances where God is described as speaking. He talked with Adam and Eve both before and after the fall (Genesis 1:28–30; 3:9–19). Then there is God's call to Abram (Genesis 12:1–3), followed by long conversations between him and God (for example, in Genesis 15:1–21; 17:1–21). We are all acquainted with the extensive dialogues between Moses and God at the burning bush (Exodus 3:1–4:23) and the revelations of God to His prophets. In each of these instances God is portrayed as communicating with people in actual spoken words, not simply through general ideas. Human language is never viewed as a barrier in divine-human communication.

The distinguishing characteristic of a true prophet is that he does not speak his own words but the words of God (Deuteronomy 18:18–20). God says repeatedly, "I will put My words in his mouth." This accounts for the fact that prophets often spoke for God in the first person!

Nathan, for example, could say to David, on God's behalf, "I will also appoint a place for My people Israel and will plant them, that they may live in their own place and not be disturbed. . . . I will raise up your descendant after you, who will come forth from you, and I will establish his kingdom" (2 Samuel 7:10, 12). Similarly, other prophets claimed to speak God's words in the first person (see, for example, 1 Kings 20:13; 2 Kings 17:13; 2 Chronicles 12:5).

Isaiah, too, was so overcome by his message that he lapsed into the first person, as though it were God Himself who was speaking. He began by telling the story of a vineyard owner who was disappointed that his best efforts did not produce grapes. Then, without further explanation, he launched into a speech given by the vineyard owner: "And now, O inhabitants of Jerusalem and men of Judah, judge between Me and My vineyard. What more was there to do for My vineyard that I have not done in it?" (Isaiah 5:3–4). Obviously, Isaiah was not the owner of the vineyard; he was just breaking forth with God's message. He spoke on God's behalf.

The prophets claimed incredible authority! Ponder the words of Samuel to Saul: "You have acted foolishly; you have not kept the commandment of the Lord your God, which He commanded you, for now the Lord would have established your kingdom over Israel forever. But now your kingdom shall not endure" (1 Samuel 13:13–14). This judgment came to Saul because he did not obey the previous message that had come through Samuel's lips. *To disobey what Samuel had said was to disobey God!*

There are other ways that the Bible affirms that the words of Scripture are the words of God. For example, David is the author of Psalm 2, which speaks about the heathen being in a rage and the nations being "in an uproar" (v. 1). Yet when the apostles quoted this psalm in a prayer, they ascribed David's words to God, "who by the Holy Spirit, through the mouth of our father David Your servant, said" (Acts 4:25). When David was speaking, the Holy Spirit was speaking.

Finally, consider the descriptions of God's Word found in the Old Testament. Musing on the despair over the un-faithfulness of people, David declared, "The words of the Lord are *pure* words; as silver tried in a furnace on the earth, refined seven times" (Psalm 12:6, emphasis added). The Hebrew word *pure* means freedom from imperfections and impurities. This claim is made for speech that came from God to the prophet, but can be applied to all "Words of the Lord."

"As for God, His way is blameless; the word of the Lord is *tried;* He is a shield to all who take refuge in Him" (Psalm 18:30, emphasis added). That word *tried* means flawless. The same thought is repeated in Psalm 119:140: "Your word is very pure, therefore Your servant loves it."

The Old Testament repeatedly claims to be the Word of God, and those words are therefore as enduring as God Himself: "Forever, O Lord, Your word is settled in heaven" (Psalm 119:89). And again, "The grass withers, the flower fades, but the word of our God stands forever" (Isaiah 40:8).

If you call the authors of the Old Testament to the witness stand, they will affirm with one voice, "We are speaking the words that have been given to us by God."

The implications, as we shall see, are staggering.

THE CLAIMS OF
THE NEW TESTAMENT

New Testament writers have the same ring of authority. They cited the Old Testament as the Word of God and put their own letters on the same level.

God spoke directly out of heaven at least three times during Christ's ministry on earth: at the baptism of Jesus, at the transfiguration, and even when Christ groaned in agony as He approached the crucifixion. Jesus, you remember, was troubled in spirit and prayed that He might be saved from the impending hour of trial (John 12:27). Yet, more important, He desired that the Father be glorified (v. 28). The heavens responded, "Then a voice came out of heaven: 'I have both glorified it, and will glorify it again'" (v. 28). Yes, God can speak, and does. The authors claimed that they were both recording and writing God's Word out of their own experience.

Paul, who authored at least thirteen books of the New Testament, claimed to have received revelations from God and wrote what he was told to say.

- "If anyone thinks he is a prophet or spiritual, let him recognize that the things which I write to you are the Lord's commandment. But if anyone does not recognize this, he is not recognized" (1 Corinthians 14:37–38).
- "For this reason we also constantly thank God that when you received the word of God which you heard from us, you accepted it not as the word of men, but for what it really is, the word of God, which also performs its work in you who believe" (1 Thessalonians 2:13).
- "For this we say to you by the word of the Lord, that we who are alive and remain until the coming of the Lord, will not precede those who have fallen asleep" (1 Thessalonians 4:15).

Peter made a direct link between the word that he was preaching and the unchangeable words of the Old Testament.

- "For you have been born again not of seed which is perishable but imperishable, that is, through the living and enduring word of God. For, 'All flesh is like grass, and all its glory like the flower of grass. The grass withers, and the flower falls off, but the word of the Lord endures forever.' And this is the word which was preached to you" (1 Peter 1:23–25; cf. Isaiah 40:6–8).

John claimed that the visions that comprise the book of Revelation are the words of the Lord and warned that if anyone added to these words, "God will add to him the plagues which are written in this book; and if anyone takes away from the words of the book of this prophecy, God will take away his part from the tree of life and from the holy city, which are written in this book" (Revelation 22:18–19). For Paul, Peter, and John to have made such claims for what they wrote would have been sheer madness unless, of course, they were, in fact, speaking the words of God.

What if we were to systematically page through the Bible, listing all of the instances in which it claims to be of divine origin? Either directly or indirectly we would find some fifteen hundred statements that claim its divine origin. The sixty-six books speak with a consistent voice that these are the words of God.

Still, accusations fly of deception on the part of biblical authors, even if they don't stick: "Many of the claimed fulfilled prophecies in scriptures were actually made after the prophesized [sic] events took place," writes one atheist professor, though he doesn't explain how the writers could have pulled that off.[1]

To say that the writers were either deceived or lying just does not wash. If so, the Bible is surely the most fraudulent book that has ever been written! It would be a matter of incomprehensible irony that the very book that has inspired the highest standard of morality, the book that has given the world the most coherent worldview, the book that has given us a Christ who is admired even by skeptics—that this book is based on multiplied deceptions is beyond belief.

In effect, God signed every page of the Bible. We have every reason to believe that His signature was not forged. God has spoken and He has told us so.

THE UNITY OF THE BIBLE

Joseph Smith claims to have received a message from an angel and thus the Book of Mormon came to be. But his claims are suspect for at least two reasons. First, the Book of Mormon has been shown to be hopelessly untrustworthy at every point of its history; not a single geographical site recorded has been discovered nor has any event in the book had independent confirmation. Second, there are no other prophets who claimed to have a revelation that was consistent with his. The Book of Mormon has but one author, a man who plagiarized much of his material and whose personal character is suspect. Subjected to the same kind of evaluation, Muhammad, the author of the Qur'an, would fare no better.

In contrast, the Bible is really a library of sixty-six books written by about forty different authors over a period that spans fifteen hundred years. If one of the most important characteristics of truth is consistency, we must ask, does the Bible present a unified story line? Since God's message cannot contradict itself, we must investigate whether the sixty-six books each tell a separate story, or whether they present one story told in sixty-six different ways. In other words, if we were to put the Bible on the witness stand and scrutinize it for consistency, how would it fare?

The Unity of Authorship

Consistency is not the only test for truth, but it is one of the most important. Prosecuting attorneys tell us that a lie can seldom withstand close scrutiny. Under cross-examination the words of a witness will almost always either be confirmed or come unraveled. If the truth is not told, at some point it will simply not "add up."

Obviously, a purely human book can also be consistent. A book on, say, physics, astronomy, or biology can be free of contradictions. Such books can present a unified view of the subject at hand. But the unity of the Bible is much more remarkable for the following reasons.

Consider:

- It evolved over a period of fifteen centuries, written in three different languages. During this period empires rose and fell and cultures came and went, but this did not affect the unity of the Bible. The intricacy of its message and history simply could not have been orchestrated by a man or a group of men.
- It was written by forty different human authors. These came from a variety of occupations: kings, fishermen, tax collectors, shepherds, prophets, and even a physician. In all it would be difficult to find a more diverse collection of writers. They run the gamut from Moses, who was highly educated, to Peter, who was a fisherman. Though

they wrote at different periods of world history, their writings dovetail with one another, not superficially, but intricately and brilliantly.

- The books were penned under different circumstances and in different countries and cultures, such as were in Asia, Africa, and Europe. Paul wrote from a dungeon in Rome, James wrote from Jerusalem, Moses from the Sinai, and Daniel from Babylon.

- The Bible discusses diverse theological matters, such as the nature of God and His purposes, the characteristics of both good and evil angels, and the nature of man and God's plan of redemption. It would be difficult enough to get ten men to agree on so much as one single theological issue, much less forty men agreeing on matters about which others can only speculate.

Imagine, say, a book on medicine written by forty different authors over a period of fifteen centuries. And yet, also imagine that the book is so up-to-date that it can still cure the sick today! Surely, we would have to admit that such agreement is remarkable. But the Bible treats subjects that are even more controversial and further removed from personal investigation. Yet it treats these matters with authority and unity.

Of course, in some instances the biblical writers had the opportunity of knowing what some of the previous authors had written. Malachi probably was acquainted with the other sacred books of the Old Testament. But Daniel might not have known what Ezekiel had written, and many of the prophets would not have known the message their contemporaries were giving. In the New Testament, Paul wrote independently of John; James did not know what Paul was writing.

If there had been collusion, if the writers would have consciously attempted to make their writings agree with others, there would have been a superficial unity and apparent inconsistencies would have been resolved. *The fact that the Bible has unity despite obvious differences in content, style, and perspective is a powerful witness to the independence of each author.*

The Unity of Theme

The biblical writers selected what they wrote in light of the overall theme they intended to convey. The Bible is not a collection of books on many different topics; there is only one theme, and that is the topic of Christ and the redemption He provided.

The book of Genesis begins with creation, the fall of man, and God's plan to redeem at least a part of humanity from the effects of human rebellion. Thus we might say that the theme of the Bible can be stated in two words: *sin* and the *grace* of the coming Redeemer. Right after the fall, God promised, "I will put enmity between you and the woman, and between your seed and her seed; He shall bruise you on the head, and you shall bruise him on the heel" (Genesis 3:15). The entire Old Testament grows out of this initial prophecy.

Of course there are subthemes: the providence of God in His dealings with His people, the matter of suffering from God's viewpoint, and the origin and destination of Satan. But all of these are played out against the background of God's dealings with fallen humanity. The Bible does not have sixty-six stories to tell, but one story of God's response to man's rebellion.

Christ confirmed that the theme of the Bible was His

own coming. Engaged in controversy with the Jews, He said, "Search the scriptures; for in them ye think ye have eternal life: and they are they which testify of me" (John 5:39 KJV). And again, "Had ye believed Moses, ye would have believed me; for he wrote of me" (v. 46 KJV). He frequently referred to Scripture as pointing to Himself. He indicted the nation for rejecting Him (Matthew 21:42–46; cf. Psalm 118:22–23). Luther was right when he said, "Christ is involved in the Scriptures as a body in its clothes."

Walking with the disciples en route to Emmaus He said, "'O foolish men and slow of heart to believe in all that the prophets have spoken! Was it not necessary for the Christ to suffer these things and to enter into His glory?' Then beginning with Moses and with all the prophets, He explained to them the things concerning Himself in all the Scriptures" (Luke 24:25–27). Later He added, "These are My words which I spoke to you while I was still with you, *that all things which are written about Me in the Law of Moses and the Prophets and the Psalms must be fulfilled*" (v. 44, emphasis added).

The apostles saw Christ as the center of the Scriptures. At Pentecost, Peter used Psalm 16:8–11 and Psalm 110:1 as the basis of his proclamation of the risen Christ (Acts 2:25–36). And when Philip met the Ethiopian eunuch he "preached Jesus to him" (Acts 8:35).

From the earliest expression of the gospel in Genesis 3:15 until the "Even so, come, Lord Jesus!" of Revelation 22:20 (NKJV), the Bible has an integrated story line. Like a garment woven with many different threads but all contributing to the shape of the whole, so the Bible has sixty-six books all contributing to one grand design.

The Reformers also saw Christ as the unifying theme of the Bible. Luther said, "All Scripture teaches nothing but the cross." Calvin affirmed, "Christ cannot be properly known in any other way than from the Scriptures."

To quote Pascal, "Jesus Christ, whom the two testaments regard, the Old as its hope, the New as its model, and both as their center."[2]

The Unity of Structure

"The New is in the Old concealed; the Old is in the New Revealed" is a statement that is often heard. There are some 180 quotations from the Old Testament in the New Testament. This is in addition to references to Old Testament characters and events. The whole Old Testament points toward a future day when God will personally redeem fallen humanity. We cannot separate the two testaments without mutilating the whole. As Floyd Hamilton said, "In its structure the Bible is a unit, each part interlaced with and interpreted by the other parts, so that every part is necessary for a complete understanding of the whole."[3]

This unity is achieved despite a diverse literary structure that includes "history, law (civil, criminal, ethical, ritual, sanitary), religious poetry, didactic treatises, lyric poetry, parable and allegory, biography, personal correspondence, personal memoirs and diaries, in addition to the distinctively Biblical types of prophecy and apocalyptic. . . . For all that there is a unity which binds the whole together."[4]

This unity is so precise it defies human wisdom. For example, in Genesis 1:1 we read, "In the beginning God created the heavens and the earth." The word *God* is a *plural* noun; although the text teaches that there is only one God, the plural noun leaves room for a belief in the Trinity, which will be revealed later in the Scriptures.

And yet despite the unity there is also diversity. The

authors of Scripture are not just individually repeating the same things. They consider the great truths God has revealed, but from different standpoints. L. Gaussen said that the books of the Bible are like the instruments of a skilled musician, who takes up a funeral flute, the shepherd's pipe, or the trumpet that summons to battle. Just so, God chose, as it were, a variety of instruments that He inspired by the breath of His Spirit. Like an organist who can elicit both tears and cheers by using his or her skillful gifts, so God has communicated with different moods and different sounds. God communicated with the harmony and diversity of a symphony orchestra.[5]

The God of the Old Testament is the same as the God of the New. Liberal theories that teach that the God of the Old Testament is harsh and cruel, whereas the God of the New is loving and tolerant, simply do not hold up in the face of the unity of the Bible. Just read the warnings of Christ, or even better, read the descriptions of God's judgment in the book of Revelation. God has not changed His mind about homosexuality, adultery, or rebellion in general. In this age, judgment is not meted out directly, but rather stored up for future retribution. If you are unconvinced, just read 2 Thessalonians 1:6–9. It is unthinkable that the God of the Old Testament is less tolerant than the God of the New, for He is the Lord and does "not change" (see Malachi 3:6). The character of God in both Testaments is one and the same.

The Unity of Symbolism

In the Old Testament fire is symbolic of purification and judgment; water is often symbolic of the Holy Spirit, as is oil. In both Testaments leaven is symbolic of evil. It was taken out of the Jewish homes in preparation for the Passover; and

Christ warned His disciples to be aware of the "leaven of the Pharisees and Sadducees" (Matthew 16:6).

Or consider the relationship between the Old Testament book of Leviticus and the New Testament book of Hebrews; or the intimate relationship between Daniel and Revelation. Here the typography and symbolism display a fit that is as carefully crafted as a glove that fits the hand. Yet each later book goes much beyond its Old Testament counterpart.

Imagine various pieces of a cathedral arriving from different countries and cities, converging on a central location. In fact, imagine that investigation proves that forty different sculptors made contributions over a period of many centuries. Yet the pieces fit together to form a single magnificent structure. Would this not be proof that behind the project was a single mind, one designer who used His workmen to sculpt a well-conceived plan?

The Bible is that cathedral, assembled by one superintelligent architect.

THE DECISION YOU CANNOT AVOID

The evidence presented in this chapter about the Bible's unity despite its diversity constitutes a *logical* reason why I believe the Bible is God's Word because I am forced to make a decision: *The Bible is either true, or it is a forgery; it is either a good book or an indescribably bad book; it is either the Word of God or the misleading, deceptive words of men.* Let us not fall into the illogical views of those liberals who say that the Bible is not the Word of God, but nevertheless is a helpful guide for the church to follow. It is either a fact or a fraud.

I can't say it more clearly: If the Bible is mistaken regarding its own origin, we have no reason to think it is reliable about anything else. We do not have the luxury to pick and choose what we consider to be from God and what is not; and if the authors were writing their own ideas, not a single line should be taken seriously. If they were so deceived regarding the source of their ideas, they would have been deceived about the content of those ideas. If the Bible is wrong fifteen hundred times, it collapses like a house of cards.

There is no use trying to put a good face on this by saying, "The authors were essentially good men who believed they were speaking for God, but they were mistaken." If they so easily confused their own words with God's words, they were either deceivers or deceived. We have no way of knowing where their delusions end.

For years liberals have striven to make the Bible a purely human book. They have attempted to strip it of its miracles, to reinterpret its divine teachings so as to adapt it to the syncretism of our age. Pains have been made to remake Christ into a mere man, no matter how badly the text of the New Testament had to be mutilated. And yet they have wanted to believe that the Bible does contain at least some reliable information about God; they have treated Christ with admiration and have pointed to the cross as a demonstration of the love of God. They tell us that they want to treat the Bible with "reverence" rather than "slavish literalism." But if the Bible is wrong about its origin, reverence is woefully out of place.

Imagine a biography of Winston Churchill in which the author repeatedly says, "Churchill said to me . . ." Then we discover that the author had never met Churchill, much less had a conversation with him. Of what value would the book be? It would enlighten us more about the author's own delusions than it would about Churchill. We could hardly take the book seriously.

Let those who reject the Bible as the Word of God do so if they wish, but they cannot have it both ways. If the claims to its origin are false, let us at least have the courage to admit it is fraudulent and loudly discredit it at every opportunity.

On the other hand, if the claims of the Bible are in fact true, it is obvious that it would be without error in the original manuscripts. If God is a God of truth, He must speak only that which is consistent with His character. It would be unthinkable to have an untruthful message from a truthful God. To say, as some do, that the Bible is authoritative in matters of theology but has errors in matters of history and science, is nonsense. (This is so important it will be developed more fully in the next chapter.)

Finally, if the Bible is true, at least some of the mysteries of our existence can be solved. For God has chosen to tell us truths about Himself we could discover in no other way. God has spoken, and we finally have some hope that we can push ahead with our knowledge of Him.

Let us open the shutters and let the sun shine in. "The unfolding of Your words gives light; it gives understanding to the simple" (Psalm 119:130).

FOR FURTHER CONSIDERATION

How Much Evidence Is Proof?

Can we *prove* that the Bible is the Word of God? Throughout this book various reasons will be given to accept the Bible as the Word of God. But it is certainly possible that a skeptic who reads this book might remain unconvinced. He or she might be looking for a kind of "proof" that is unavailable.

First, we must keep in mind that there are very few things

in life that are proven in an absolute sense. We all know that 2 + 2 = 4 is a proposition that needs no proof because it is self-evident to the person who understands the meaning of the terms. But mathematics is about the only discipline in which we have such certainty.

Other kinds of knowledge are always dependent on observation and experience. When all of the evidence is in, we can say that we have "proved" a proposition, but even then there might be exceptions. Scientists who have studied thousands of snowflakes tell us that there are no two that are alike. We might say that they have "proved" that this is so. But of course, a moment's reflection tells us that this proposition cannot be proved absolutely, because there could be exceptions. Think of the hundreds of billions of snowflakes that have never been compared to one another! At the end of the day, only an omniscient being who knows all things can say absolutely, "No two snowflakes are alike."

When it comes to historical documents, the evidence is even more subject to interpretation and possible misidentification. The statement "Winston Churchill was prime minister of England" has substantially better verification than the statement "Julius Caesar ruled in Rome." Obviously, the more recent an event and the more witnesses, the more credibility can be given to such accounts.

Arguments based on history can be discounted even in the face of highly reliable evidence. Questions about the credibility of the witnesses, the accuracy of their statements, and the trustworthiness of the copies of the manuscripts can always be raised. The simple fact is that arguments from history can never provide evidence that is "foolproof." After all, history cannot be repeated. None of us was a witness to God's creation of the heavens and the earth. Thus, there is always room for competing theories.

In the case of the Bible, the question of "proof" becomes even more intriguing. Here is a book that not only speaks about matters of history and morals, but also pointedly reveals the subtle deceptions of the human heart. That is why *the most compelling reason I believe the Bible to be the Word of God is one that is available only to those who have a desire to submit to its authority.* To quote the words of Christ, "If any one is willing to do His will, he will know of the teaching, whether it is of God or whether I speak from Myself" (John 7:17). Without the *willing*, there cannot be the knowing.

The reason for this is not difficult to grasp: the Bible reveals doctrines that exist outside the realm of human observation. It analyzes our personal predicament and brings a conviction of sin that makes us uncomfortable. Indeed, Christ said that by nature we prefer spiritual darkness to spiritual light, and thus will hide from God's revelation whenever it is convenient. Left to ourselves, we resist the Bible's teachings and will believe as little of it as we possibly can, refusing to take the next step of faith.

Also, historical studies can only take us so far; faith must take us the rest of the way. Even if historical studies can marshal impressive evidence to show that Christ died on a Roman cross, historical investigation cannot verify that He "died for our sins" as Christians believe.

After a lecture I gave at a university defending the resurrection of Christ, a philosophy professor asked, "Even if I grant your argument that Christ arose from the dead, how does this prove that He was the Son of God, and a Savior?" He went on to suggest that Christ might have discovered a secret on how to make Himself alive, a secret that scientists might discover in the future. No matter how far-fetched his rationale, this illustrates the difficulty of "proving" that the Bible is the Word of God. Such skeptics will not be convinced by this book, nor, I fear, by any other that seeks to defend the reasonableness of Christianity.

No matter how much evidence for the credibility of the Bible is accumulated, I must stress once more that Christ must still be received by faith. I do not mean blind faith, nor faith that is contrary to logic, but rather faith based on reasonable evidence. Yet it is faith nevertheless. If arguments for Christianity were absolute, no faith would be needed. All that we would have to do is point to the evidence, and reasonable people would *have* to believe.

Our own experience proves that we are slow to accept what the Bible has to say about us and our relationship with God. Indeed, not one of us can make the transition from doubt to faith on our own. Christ taught, and the rest of the New Testament confirms, that only by the power of God's Spirit can such a transformation be brought about. "No one can come to Me unless the Father who sent Me draws him; and I will raise him up on the last day" (John 6:44), Christ taught. In other words, when we come to transfer our trust to Christ alone for our salvation, it is not merely by historical investigation, but by the action of God's Spirit.

This is not to be interpreted as accepting modern subjectivism that says, "I know I'm right because I feel (or think) that I am, and no one can take my private beliefs from me!" We become convinced that the Bible is the Word of God, not by subjective hunches, but by having our subjective hunches destroyed when we are humbled in the presence of the God revealed on the pages of the Bible. We finally come to realize that this Book is telling the painful truth about ourselves and our relationships in the world. The pieces of life's puzzle suddenly come together and we are led to say, "Once I was blind but now I see."

The Bible is a mirror, not a photograph. A mirror shows us as we are; we can't add more hair, a bit of robust color, and with a slight of hand, remove all blemishes. No wonder the Bible frightens those who are unwilling to face their sins but is a balm to those who are finally prepared to own up to their need and accept the redemption of Christ.

A friend of mine who grew up in an atheistic home ventured into the New Age movement to satisfy his hunger and restlessness. From there it was into the occult and even embracing "white supremacy" as his compelling philosophy. But when he was exposed to the Bible, he wrote, "To my amazement, all of my flawed theories of white supremacy were no match for His loving Spirit, and I soon found myself unable to stomach the creeds that I once thought were self-evident. No one argued with me to prove me wrong. *Intellectual battlements were like puffs of smoke before His breath.*"

One of my prayer partners likes to tell the story of how he watched television preachers "just for laughs." He could not believe that there were people who actually believed in the creation of Adam and Eve and the virgin birth. But the more he listened, the more curious he became and the more anxious to read the Bible for himself. When the truth of his own sinfulness and need of a Savior dawned on him, he was converted. "After that," he said, "I realized that the God who saved me could certainly have created Adam and Eve and most assuredly could have had His Son born of a virgin." Once his heart was changed, his mind was changed.

Those skeptics who are open to the possibility that God has intervened in history, those men and women who have a desire to know the truth even if it challenges their self-perception, might find this book a path to faith. By understanding the reasonableness of the Bible, they may be led to give it an honest hearing. They might find their curiosity stimulated, their appetites whetted, and their hearts turned toward Christ, the center of the biblical faith. The Spirit of God will use the Word of God to bring about a transformation that is the gateway to eternal life.

Those who are confronted with the growing conviction that the Christ of the Bible is the Son of God will find that their intellectual barriers will be overcome by an awareness that He is the "truth." Historical and scientific matters that were previously a stumbling block in accepting the Bible will fall into place. Those who have discovered that the Bible is telling the truth about themselves are quite convinced it tells the truth about other matters also.

In sum, God uses the Bible to break through the natural barriers erected against its claims. The gift of enlightenment and the transforming power of the Holy Spirit enable men, women, and children to embrace Christ as their own. "In the exercise of His will He brought us forth by the word of truth, so that we would be a kind of first fruits among His creatures" (James 1:18).

Thus, this book is written with two prayers. First, that those who believe might understand the reasonableness of their faith. Evidence will be presented to show why critics who attack the Bible are wrongheaded. In short, we need to be able to defend the faith "once for all entrusted to God's holy people" (Jude 1:3 NIV). Our faith is well placed, for the Bible can be trusted.

Second, I pray that the most radical skeptic who has dismissed the Bible as folklore will read these pages. Hopefully, these arguments will lead the skeptic to study the Scriptures he or she has long since abandoned, and God will graciously grant the ability to know and believe that "God was in Christ reconciling the world to Himself" (2 Corinthians 5:19). If you are a skeptic, exposure to the Bible should be your first assignment.

Surely, no one ever spoke like Christ, who stands at the center of the Bible. These words alone are enough to make us ponder His incredible authority. "All things have been handed over to Me by My Father; and no one knows the Son except the Father; nor does anyone know the Father except the Son, and anyone to whom the Son wills to reveal Him" (Matthew 11:27).

Let's continue the journey.

HISTORY CONFIRMS THE BIBLE'S RELIABILITY

Glance through the Bible and you will encounter stories about men like Abraham, Moses, and David. You will read about Christ, His disciples, and Paul. The Bible is filled with thousands of events that purport to have actually happened in the continuum we call history. Births, deaths, hardships, and miracles —they all are there.

But is this history reliable?

It depends on whom you ask. *Time* magazine quotes John Van Seters of the University of North Carolina as saying, "There was no Moses, no crossing of the sea, no revelation on Mount Sinai." Indeed, *Time* reported that Seters spoke to the Society of Biblical Literature with "Pope-like confidence."[1]

Time editorialized that years of searching for evidence have "convinced all but the most conservative experts that Abraham and the rest of the patriarchs were inventions of the Bible's authors."[2] In keeping with this viewpoint, Peter Jennings, in an ABC network television special on Jerusalem, commented on the Jewish, Muslim, and Christian belief in Abraham and then asked, "What can historians tell us about him?" His answer: "They don't even know whether Abraham lived."

How can we believe the Bible is historically reliable in the face of such sweeping denials? Must we simply look the other way and keep believing, no matter how mythical the Bible really is? Worse, should we close our eyes to what these scholars say, hoping that their radical views will just evaporate?

There is a better way.

Let's take a moment to understand the deeply held convictions of liberal biblical scholars. They, like the rest of us, bring their own basic presuppositions to the study of the Bible, and these determine the outcome of their investigations. Two nonnegotiable dogmas are held by them at all costs.

First, none of the Bible is accepted without independent confirmation from history and archaeology. These scholars speak of themselves as "minimalists," meaning that they accept only the bare minimum of the Bible, limiting themselves to what secular sources can confirm. For example, since no reference to the Exodus has been found in extrabiblical sources (that is, sources outside of the Bible), the event is not to be believed. For years many scholars did not believe in the existence of King David until his name was discovered in two inscriptions. Now it is fashionable to believe that he was indeed a king of Israel, thanks to recent discoveries. But since Abraham has not yet been independently confirmed, it is assumed that the biblical story is a fabrication.

We should notice in passing that no other historical documents are held with such skepticism. Ancient manuscripts are usually accepted at face value, along with archaeological inscriptions and the like. Although these seldom are thought to need independent confirmation, the Bible is different. If some other documents do not confirm it, its history is denied; if such documents contradict it, the Bible is assumed to be in error.

Second, there is the deeply held conviction that no miracles can have occurred. Even if some scholars now believe David lived, they most assuredly do not believe that he spoke under the inspiration of the Holy Spirit or that God made a personal covenant with him. They would scoff at the story about David's encounter with an avenging angel on the threshing floor of Araunah the Jebusite.

Did Christ exist? Although Christ was referred to thirteen times in contemporary secular literature, one scholar nevertheless does not believe He existed. He reasons that "no 1st century inscription mentions him and no object or building has survived which has a specific link to him."[3] Thus totally disregarding the excellent New Testament manuscript evidence, the conclusion is that there was no Jesus, at least no Jesus that resembles the one in whom Christians believe. No wonder the Bible of the critics is so thin, filled with bits and pieces of history, history that is reduced to conform to prior assumptions.

To repeat: Some scholars will accept nothing in the Bible unless it is independently confirmed. Since the crucifixion of Christ is not mentioned in other histories, it is generally denied. And even if a first-century reference to the crucifixion of

Christ were discovered, these critics would certainly not admit to the biblical interpretation of this event. They would give grudging acceptance to whatever historical-archaeological studies might yield, but not a mite more.

Those of us who believe that the Bible is trustworthy look at matters very differently. We've already learned that we must either accept the Bible as the Word of God or reject it *in toto* as a forgery. And because we accept the Bible as the Word of God, we do not suspend belief until biblical events are confirmed by archaeology. We believe that the Exodus happened even if the Egyptians didn't record it (What makes us think that such a proud people would record a defeat for their nation anyway?). We believe that a big fish swallowed Jonah long before a zoologist measured the gullet of a whale and told us that such a feat is possible.

We acknowledge historical problems in the text, but we also believe—and this is important—that if all of the facts were known, the Bible's history would be accurate even in minor details. We strongly disagree with those who say, "Well, the Bible is a religious document, so who cares whether it has historical errors?" Religion, if it is worth believing, must be based on facts. Yes, there is room for faith, but unless it is faith in facts, faith is not only useless, but also destructive.

If a book, say, on World War I had some errors, it might not affect the book as a whole. The author might have written a rather competent history, but some of the information was limited, or the author's perspective skewed. Some of the sources might be suspect, and yet with proper evaluation, the rest of the work might have merit.

Not so with the Bible.

The Bible is not just a book on history, but also a book on *doctrine,* a book that takes us beyond the realm of human speculation. We have already learned that it claims to be the Word of God more than fifteen hundred times. If it has some historical errors, it might well have some theological errors too. If Moses didn't cross the Red Sea, why should we believe that God gave the Ten Commandments on Sinai? If Abraham did not rescue Lot from tribal kings, as critics used to teach, then we cannot trust the story of God's covenant with Abraham. If the Bible names the wrong Roman ruler when the decree was given for Joseph to return to Bethlehem, why should we believe in the virgin birth? Remember, it is either all true, or it is riddled with errors.

In addition, biblical history and biblical theology are often so closely entwined we cannot separate one from the other. Is the crucifixion of Christ a historical event, or is it a doctrinal event? Of course it is both. The same can be said for the fall of man in Eden, the Exodus, the giving of the Law, and the resurrection of Christ.

The Bible cannot afford to have historical errors. We are encouraged to believe its doctrines because of the reliability of its history. Christ challenged Nicodemus, "If I have told you earthly things and you do not believe, how can you believe if I tell you heavenly things?" (John 3:12 esv). When God speaks He is just as reliable about the earthly things as He is about the heavenly! In fact, the reliability of the earthly matters gives us confidence in the reliability of the heavenly matters that are beyond the realm of human investigation.

Think this through.

To a paralytic Christ said, "Son, your sins are forgiven" (Mark 2:5). Predictably, Christ's critics scoffed, saying, "Why does this man speak that way? He is blaspheming; who can forgive sins but God alone?" (v. 7).

Christ, knowing what they were thinking, asked a

challenging question: "Which is easier, to say to the paralytic, 'Your sins are forgiven'; or to say, 'Get up, and pick up your pallet and walk'?" (v. 9).

How would you have answered? Obviously it is easier to *say,* "Your sins are forgiven," simply because talk is cheap and there is no way to prove that the person's sins have not been taken away. No one has ever seen sins leave a human body; the act of salvation cannot be empirically verified. A priest might tell a parishioner that his sins are forgiven and there is no way to disprove it.

But if you or I were to say "Rise, and walk" that is an entirely different matter. We had better have the power to back up our words with a visible miracle! Forgiving sins takes more authority than healing a sick man, but Christ is talking about making *claims;* it is easier to *claim* to forgive sins than it is to raise a paralytic from his bed.

Don't miss the clincher: "'But so that you may know that the Son of Man has authority on earth to forgive sins'—He said to the paralytic—'I say to you, get up, pick up your pallet and go home'" (vv. 10–11). Immediately the man was healed and took up his pallet and went home (read Mark 2:1–12).

Christ's point: My authority to perform a *visible* miracle gives credence to My authority to perform an *invisible* one! My *earthly authority proves My heavenly authority.* Here we have a historical event that is the basis for a doctrinal claim.

The bottom line is that the Bible has to be reliable about the things of this earth if we are to believe it about the things of heaven. We cannot let the biblical writers off the hook, making excuses for their failures. In their case, even a few minor errors would be fatal to the whole document.

So, is the Bible historically reliable? Let us look at the available evidence.

THE CONTRIBUTION
OF ARCHAEOLOGY

Archaeology can be defined as "a study based on the excavation, decipherment and critical evaluation of the records of the past as they affect the Bible."[4] The last fifty years have been a bonanza for archaeologists.

Obviously, archaeology is very limited in what it can prove and cannot prove. It is unrealistic to think that it can reconstruct all the ancient history of the Middle East. Of the hundreds of places mentioned in the Bible, many, but not all, have been identified. We cannot expect archaeology to solve every historical problem encountered in the Bible.

Second, archaeology is not an exact science. It is often fragmentary, disjointed, and subject to interpretation. We are grateful for those who have studied the customs, utensils, and building materials of various civilizations to throw light on biblical culture. We are thankful for every clue left behind as civilizations came and went. But archaeologists sometimes differ among themselves as to how all this data should be understood.

Years ago when I spent a summer studying in Jerusalem, an archaeological group returned from Ai to tell us that they were ready to "rewrite the book of Joshua." They claimed to have uncovered evidence that Joshua's account of the conquest was incorrect, and they now could improve on his history! These students thought they had more knowledge 3,400 years *after* the fact than a man who *saw* it all happen! One noted archaeologist disagreed with these students and even believed they were digging at the wrong tell. (A tell is an artificial hill created by various levels of debris from ancient cities that were destroyed and rebuilt.)

Those of us who believe the Bible is God's Word will

be neither surprised nor shaken when a particular archaeological discovery appears to contradict the Bible. Usually, further research points toward the reliability of the biblical record. Of course, if the Bible were entirely off base, if it were inconsistent with the known course of Middle East history, if it spoke of mythological cities, and if it scrambled historical time lines that have been established by independent historical research, we would humbly admit that the Bible is unreliable from cover to cover.

To the contrary, the majority of archaeological finds have illuminated biblical history and have, if anything, confirmed the biblical record. If we were to make a list of discoveries that have shut the mouths of biblical critics, it would be long indeed. Given the Bible's excellent reliability over the long haul, it is doubtful if archaeology could ever make a discovery that would conclusively prove the Bible in error.

Though our faith is not dependent on the next archaeological find, it is gratifying to know that, as time moves on, more and more discoveries confirm the biblical record. Unbelievers must grudgingly admit that archaeology has proved to be a friend of the Bible, not its foe.

Dr. Henry Morris, a Christian apologist and scientist, has written, "It must be extremely significant that, in view of the great mass of corroborative evidence regarding the biblical history of these periods, there exists today not one unquestionable find of archaeology that proves the Bible to be in error at any point."[5] *The New International Dictionary of Biblical Archaeology,* written by a score of experts in various fields, says in the preface that archaeology has demonstrated the historical and geographical reliability of the Bible. "It is now known, for instance, that, along with the Hittites, Hebrew scribes were the best historians in the entire ancient

Near East, despite contrary propaganda that emerged from Assyria, Egypt and elsewhere."[6]

Most remarkable is the fact that the peoples, places, and events mentioned in the Bible are found just where the Scriptures locate them. As Hamilton wrote, "The Scriptures are an exact representation of the reality and not clumsy attempts to reconstruct the setting many years after the events, at a place from it and with no accurate sources from which to draw as the critics would have us believe."[7]

Old Testament Archaeology

Where shall we begin?

Among the hundreds of archaeological finds that relate to the Old Testament, I shall confine myself to only a few. I begin with the creation account: Did Moses receive his information from God or did he simply rewrite accounts that were already in existence? A surprising archaeological discovery forces us to raise the question and answer it.

When Nineveh was excavated, thousands of clay tablets were discovered that comprised the library of King Ashurbanipal of Assyria, who reigned in the years 668–626 BC Among these writings was a set of seven tablets called the "Creation Epic" that listed six days of creation and one day of rest, which corresponds to the biblical account. Also a Babylonian creation account has been discovered, bearing some resemblance to the Genesis outline but laced with pagan polytheism and unbiblical additions.

The biblical creation account differs in these respects. First, there is the obvious difference between the many gods of paganism and the strict monotheism of the biblical account. In the Babylonian account, male and female deities give birth to other gods, and gods are fighting, cutting one another in half, making the Euphrates River flow through one eye and the Tigris River through the other. Man is created, we are told, from the blood of an evil god, mixed with clay.

Obviously, the Babylonian account is corrupt, standing in stark contrast to the sublime words, "In the beginning God created the heavens and the earth." In these words we have a description of the one God in control of His creation and the universe.

Second, the Babylonian accounts confuse matter and spirit. Indeed the initial gods are the personification of cosmic matter, and their offspring personify cosmic spaces and natural forces. In Genesis, God is depicted as being distinct from matter; He is the Creator, the Lord, independent from the world He created.

But the similarity of the order of creation cannot be accidental. Both accounts begin with primeval chaos, the beginning of light, the creation of the luminaries, and the creation of man; and on the seventh day, the Deity rests. Obviously, the accounts must have been derived from a common source.

Since the Babylonian accounts are at least a few hundred years older than Genesis, critics say that Moses derived his information from the pagan versions, taking the raw data and putting it into a theistic setting.

I suppose God could have inspired Moses to rewrite the ancient account, stripped of its polytheism, but that is unlikely. History shows that when one writer borrows an account from another, he always embellishes it, never simplifies it. As A. R. Millard put it, "All who suspect or suggest a borrowing by the Hebrews are compelled to admit large-scale revision, alteration and reinterpretation in a fashion which cannot be substantiated for any other composition from the ancient Near East or in any other Hebrew writing."[8] The Genesis account is so lofty, so straightforward and free of picturesque adornments that another explanation must be found.

A more likely scenario is that God revealed His message to previous generations, but because the account was communicated orally, it was corrupted. By the time it was written down, it was garbled with ancient religious myths and sensual innuendo. The basic outline was intact, but the record was shaped to fit the religious climate of the times. True to historical precedent, the Babylonians took the simplified account and in the retelling of the story, embellished it according to their various religious perversions.

God revealed to Moses the account as it was originally given. The Babylonian account confirms Genesis in the sense that it points to a time when the human race occupied a common home and held a common faith. *It points to a common heritage when early civilizations had a common understanding of the creation of the world.*

Interestingly, another archaeological find comes from the library of Ashurbanipal. More clay tablets have been found called the *Epic of Gilgamesh*, which records the Babylonian flood. Again, the story is told from a polytheistic point of view, namely, that the gods gave warning to a man called Utnapishtim (Mesopotamia's Noah) to build an ark and take into it the seed of all living things. The ark was built, a family was taken inside, and the flood began as scheduled. Later it came to rest on Mount Nisir, and Utnapishtim sent forth a dove, a swallow, and a raven. The dove and the swallow returned, but the raven saw that the waters were abated and did not return. When the family left the ark, Utnapishtim offered sacrifices to the gods. Interestingly, archaeology has discovered no fewer than thirty-three separate versions of this gigantic flood, only two of which do not coincide with the biblical account.[9]

Such stories tend to confirm that such a flood actually oc-curred. Obviously, as the sons of Noah spread out they would have taken the story of the flood with them. One generation told another; but because the account was verbal, each nation shaped the story to make it compatible with its own deities and worship. We should not be surprised that such accounts exist, nor should we be surprised that each account is differ-ent. When God inspired Moses to write Genesis, He gave him the authentic version.

Likewise, a monument describing the Tower of Babel was discovered in the region of Ur of Chaldees. It tells of King Ur-Nammu, who was told by his gods to build a zig-gurat (tower). This monument is some ten feet high and five feet wide. At the top is an inscription of the king setting out the tools needed for the construction. In panels beneath him men are depicted working, scaling ladders as the towers rise.

Interestingly, a clay tablet was unearthed that tells how the gods were highly offended and in a single night they destroyed what had been built, and the people were scattered abroad and their speech made strange. Again, the most rea-sonable explanation is that the story of the Tower of Babel did in fact take place.[10]

The Bible's critics have always given grudging acceptance to archaeological finds that confirm the biblical record. Here are a few examples of where critics have had to change their minds about the Bible's reliability.

- For years critics insisted that the story of Abram's rescue of Lot in Genesis 14 was not historically accurate. They said that (1) the names of the kings listed were ficti-tious, since they were not independently confirmed in secular histories; (2) the idea that the king of Babylon was serving the king of Elam was historically impossible; and (3) the story that a band of Abram's followers could have defeated the united armies of four powerful kings was absurd. But archaeology has debunked these critics. The names of some of the kings have now been identified. And there is evidence that the king of Babylon did serve the king of Elam at this time. What is more, a monument depicting a warlike expedition of the character described here was discovered, confirming that one tribe pursued another to subdue a rebellion. Abram would have been able to capture Lot and plunder some of the enemy's spoils before a larger army could recoup.[11]

- For decades it was said that the Old Testament writers invented the Hittite tribe, since their existence could not be independently confirmed. However, in 1911–1912 Professor Hugo Winckler of Berlin discovered some ten thousand clay tablets at Bogazköy, the site of the Hittite capital. The existence of the Hittite empire is now extensively proven and documented.

- The existence of Solomon's reign and his thousands of horses was at one time questioned. But in Meggido, which was one of five chariot cities, excavations have revealed the ruins of thousands of stalls for his horses and chariots (cf. 1 Kings 10:26–29).

Every month new archaeological discoveries are made. So much so, that a journal, *Biblical Archaeology Review*, is chock-full of these reports in every issue. Our understanding of biblical life and times increases year by year. And so does our confidence that the Bible is a book rooted in the soil of Middle East history, and its accounts have the marks of credibility. The Bible's geography, chronology, and its description of the rise and fall of empires all conform to the data of secular history. If the Bible is reliable in those matters where it can be tested, we have reason to believe its reliability in those matters that are beyond the present realm of investigation.

Years ago *Time* had an article on the walls of Jericho titled, "Score One for the Bible."[12] It began with the debate as to whether Joshua's capturing Jericho was fact or myth and then went on to quote archaeologist Brian Wood, who believes that Jericho's walls could have come tumbling down just at the right time to match the biblical account. We can be thankful that *Time* was willing to "Score One for the Bible." But, in the face of so much archaeological evidence that confirms the Scriptures, the caption might have read, "Score One for *Time* Magazine!"

More recently, when an archaeological discovery was purported to contradict the biblical record of Jesus' resurrection, it was soundly debunked. A film director produced a television documentary claiming that bones of Jesus and His family, including a son of Jesus, were found in an ossuary in a Jerusalem tomb. Critics pointed out that Jesus' family was too poor to afford such a tomb and burial boxes used by the rich. And one critic commented sarcastically, "Can you check the DNA of God?"

CBS News correspondent Mark Phillips reported that "although archeologists have long argued over the factual and historic accuracy of Christianity's version of history, in this case, the archeological establishment has lined up to label this claim as bunk."[13]

New Testament Archaeology

Critics have insisted that Luke's recounting of the birth of Christ is filled with historical inaccuracies. They say that Augustus did not order a census at this time and that Quirinius was governor of Syria at a later date. And, what is more, even if the census was ordered, it was not necessary for a man to go to his own city to enroll, but he could have paid the tax where he lived. And, finally, if the husband went, it was not necessary for any other member of the family to accompany him.

William Ramsey, a noted historian and archaeologist, set out to prove that Luke's history was filled with errors but emerged from his study surprised, saying, "Luke's history is unsurpassed in trustworthiness." He discovered that Cyrenius (the Greek form of Quirinius) was twice governor of Syria, first when Christ was born and again at a later period. The cycle of census shows that the approximate one recorded by Luke was in 6–5 BC, which is the commonly accepted date of Christ's birth.

Indeed, an ancient document confirmed the need for residents to return to their own cities when a census was taken. "Gaius Vivius, prefect [Roman officer] of Egypt. Because of the approaching census it is necessary for all those residing for any cause away from their own districts to prepare to return at once to their own governments, in order that they may complete the family administration of enrollment for each so that they may retain the tilled lands belonging to them."[14]

Space forbids a listing of the hundreds of times archaeology has supported or illuminated New Testament places and events. These are a few:

- The existence of the pool of Bethesda with its five porches (John 5:2).

- Pilate, whose existence was doubted, has been confirmed as a high-ranking Roman official by the discovery of "The Pilate Stone" in Caesarea.
- An altar to "an unknown god" was found in Athens (Acts 17:23).

Entire books have been written confirming the historicity of the Bible in matters related to geography, chronology, history of empires, and customs of each period.

AN EVALUATION OF NEW TESTAMENT DOCUMENTS

The best way to confirm the accuracy of the New Testament documents is to test them by the same standards used to investigate any other historical document. John Warwick Montgomery in his book *History and Christianity* spelled out three tests, derived from a book on military history that can be applied to the New Testament.[15]

First, there is the *biographical* test, which analyzes the textual tradition by which a document reaches us. This test answers the question: Since we do not have the original documents, is our present text based on reliable copies? Since there is perhaps a 250-year gap (plus or minus) between the originals and the copies that are in existence today, can we be sure that we have a reliable textual tradition?

The answer is a resounding *yes*. Listen to the words of Sir Frederic Kenyon, formerly director and principal librarian of the British Museum:

> In no other case is the interval of time between the composition of the book and date of the earliest extant

manuscripts so short as in that of the New Testament. ... We believe that we have in all essentials an accurate text of the seven extant [existing] plays of Sophocles; yet the earliest substantial manuscript upon which it is based was written more than 1,400 years after the poet's death. Aeschylus, Aristophanes, and Thucydides are in the same state; while with Euripides the interval is increased to 1,600 years. For Plato it may be put at 1,300 years, for Demosthenes as low as 1,200.[16]

And if you are still concerned about the gap of, say, 250 years, remember that we can independently confirm the text of the New Testament by (1) papyri manuscripts that were discovered in Egypt, dated as early as AD 125, containing fragments of the New Testament. Also (2) extensive quotations of the New Testament occur in the writings of the early church fathers, as further proof that the New Testament writings were known to them, possessing the same content as we have today.

Let me quote Kenyon again:

The interval, then, between the dates of the original composition and the earliest extant [existing] evidence becomes so small as to be in fact negligible, and the last foundation for any doubt that the Scriptures have come down to us substantially as they were written has now been removed. Both the authenticity and the general integrity of the books of the New Testament may be regarded as finally established.[17]

Even when we allow for the errors copyists made; even when we take into account that the various manuscripts do have minor variations, we have a reliable biblical text upon which our faith is based. No doctrine is affected by differences in spelling, word order, or the addition of an explanatory word or phrase.

The second test is *internal*, that is, the claims of the writers themselves. Do they claim to be eyewitnesses to the events recorded, or did they at least receive their information from credible sources? John claims to have been an eyewitness to the events of his gospel and explicitly says he was present at the crucifixion (John 19:35). Luke tells us that there were many accounts of the life of Christ available to him, and then he continues, "It seemed fitting for me as well, having investigated everything carefully from the beginning, to write it out for you in consecutive order, most excellent Theophilus; so that you may know the exact truth about the things you have been taught" (Luke 1:3–4).

The New Testament writers do not discredit themselves by internal contradictions or mystical ramblings. Their own moments of doubt and skepticism motivated them to search out the truth so they could write with credibility. Many of the books of the New Testament were written at a time when people were still alive who had witnessed the events that were being recorded. In some instances the writers called upon others to verify that what they were writing was correct. When Paul argued for the physical resurrection of Christ, he appealed to those who were still living who could verify this claim (1 Corinthians 15:6).

Finally, there is the *external* evidence. Do other historical materials confirm or deny the content of the documents? Here we can insert the archaeological data that was given earlier. We can also include the many quotations from the church fathers and the fact that Christ is referred to by historians such as Tacitus.

Most interesting is the fact that the famous historian Josephus referred to the resurrection of Christ.

> At this time there was a wise man called Jesus, and his conduct was good and he was known to be virtuous. ... Pilate condemned him to be crucified and die. But those who had become his disciples did not abandon his discipleship. They reported that he had appeared to them three days after his crucifixion and that he was alive.[18]

Time was quite right when it said, "Atheists can't wait to prove the whole thing is a fairy tale." But this is one fairy tale that cannot be explained away. Let us hear the words of Bernard Ramm:

> A thousand times over, the death knell of the Bible has been sounded, the funeral procession formed, the inscription cut on the tombstone, and the committal read. But somehow the corpse never stays put.
>
> No other book has been so chopped, sliced, sifted, scrutinized and vilified. What book on philosophy or religion or psychology or belles lettres of classical or modern times has been subject to such a mass attack as the Bible? with such venom and skepticism? with such thoroughness and erudition? upon every chapter, line and tenet?
>
> The Bible is still loved by millions and studied by millions.[19]

Perhaps the reason for the Bible's longevity can be found not in the men who wrote it, but in the God who inspired it. "The grass withers, the flower fades, but the word of our God stands forever" (Isaiah 40:8).

We believe the Bible when it says that Abram fought against the kings to retrieve Lot; we believe it when it says that Quirinius was governor of Syria. And we also believe it when it says, "Except a man be born again, he cannot see the kingdom of God" (John 3:3 KJV).

As already emphasized, there is more to the Christian faith than believing in the credibility of the Bible's history. To make the transition from the Bible's history to the Bible's theology requires a special act of faith, a faith that is granted by God. But if the history of the Bible were filled with errors, its doctrines would also be erroneous.

The New Testament writers knew that their faith was based on fact. Peter was an eyewitness to Christ's transfiguration and wrote, "For we did not follow cleverly devised tales when we made known to you the power and coming of our Lord Jesus Christ, but we were eyewitnesses of His majesty" (2 Peter 1:16). As this book attempts to show, there is enough evidence for those who seek, but not enough for those who take pride in their skepticism. The attitude of the heart is just as important as the reasoning of the mind.

No wonder the prophet Isaiah, facing the unbelief, idolatry, and iniquity of the people of his own day, cast a longing plea to God:

> Oh that you would rend the heavens and come down,
> that the mountains might quake at your presence . . .
> to make your name known to your adversaries,
> and that the nations might tremble at your presence!
> From of old no one has heard or perceived by the ear,
> no eye has seen a God besides you,
> who acts for those who wait for him.
> (ISAIAH 64:1, 2, 4 ESV)

FOR FURTHER CONSIDERATION

The Dead Sea Scrolls

Often we are asked: How do we know that the Bible we have in our hands has come down to us accurately? Since the manuscripts of today are copies of copies, how do we know that the text was accurately transmitted? We've already answered this question in the case of the New Testament, but what about the Old Testament?

The discovery of the Dead Sea Scrolls has confirmed that the Old Testament text has not substantially changed throughout the centuries. Here is a synopsis of perhaps the most important of all archaeological stories.

In March of 1947, a Bedouin shepherd looking for a lost goat near the Dead Sea threw a stone to ward off other animals and then heard the sound of something breaking. He found a companion and together they went into a cave where they saw several large jars containing rolls of leather and papyrus wrapped in cloths. They smuggled them across the border between Israel and Jordan that existed at the time and found an antique dealer in Bethlehem who bought them for a small fee. The merchant told a Syrian scholar in Jerusalem about them, but he was unable to identify their age or significance. The Syrian acquired several of the manuscripts and stored them in the Monastery of St. Mark in Old Jerusalem.

Realizing that these manuscripts might be of considerable value to the world, the Syrian scholar sought advice from the *École Biblique,* a French Dominican institution in Jerusalem devoted to biblical and archaeological study. A Dutch professor visited the monastery and examined one of the texts and recognized it to be an ancient copy of the prophet Isaiah. When he returned to his colleagues at *École Biblique*, they assured him that no such manuscripts of antiquity could possibly still exist, so the matter was dropped.

Eventually two librarians from the Hebrew University in Jerusalem visited the monastery and recognized that these manuscripts needed evaluation by experts in paleography (the study of ancient forms of writing). When professor E. L. Sukenik of the Hebrew University returned from America to Jerusalem in November of 1947, he realized that "this may be one of the greatest finds ever made in Palestine." So it was.

By now other scrolls had been discovered and the caves in the area were scoured for more manuscripts. In all, the caves yielded about fourteen significant finds, including one cave that housed what was believed to be a library of materials.

Where did these scrolls come from?

In 140 BC, a group of people called the Essenes left the city of Jerusalem to survive in the barren dry caves of the Judean hills. Qumran, as the site was called, was established to preserve the purity of the priesthood and to cling to the Law of Moses and the prophets.

By about AD 60 Rome became weary of the rebellion of the Jews and decided to crush them throughout the land, including the Essene community. When the Roman troops left Jericho for Qumran, the Essenes immediately hid their scrolls in nearby caves and fled to the hills, hoping to escape the wrath of the Romans. Thus these scrolls were in these caves for some two thousand years!

What is their significance?

Until these scrolls were found, the oldest Old Testament manuscripts in existence dated back to only about AD 800. These editions of the Hebrew Old Testament are known as the "Masoretic Text," so named after a group of scholars known as "Masoretes" who took great care in copying the text of the Old Testament and making sure that it corresponded with the most reliable manuscripts.

Don't be surprised that the oldest Hebrew Old Testament texts dated back to AD 800–1000. Our oldest manuscript of Plato and Aristotle goes back to only about AD 1600, and yet no one questions whether the texts we use are a faithful reproduction of what they actually wrote. The simple fact is that manuscripts do not last for century upon century, unless they are in a cool, dry place such as existed in the caves where the scrolls were found. We can be thankful that copyists took their work seriously and preserved ancient writings with meticulous care.

The next best thing to having the originals is to go back to those copies that are closest to the originals. That is what the Dead Sea Scrolls have allowed us to do.

These scrolls are some eight hundred to a thousand years older than other previously known manuscripts. Portions of every book of the Old Testament have been found except Esther. Interestingly, no writings of the Apocrypha were found. Most important was a complete scroll of the book of Isaiah. This has given scholars a wonderful opportunity to compare the text of the scrolls with the previously known texts.

The conclusions?

First, the Dead Sea Scrolls *give independent confirmation of the text of our present Old Testament books.* For example, the text of Isaiah has been shown to be substantially the same as that which is known as the Masoretic Text. Dr. Gleason L. Archer observes that the two copies of Isaiah found in the caves "proved to be word for word identical with our standard Hebrew Bible in more than 95% of the text. The 5% variation consisted chiefly of obvious slips of the pen and variations in spelling."[20]

To give a specific example:

> Of the 166 words in Isaiah 53, there are only seventeen letters [in the Qumran scroll that differ from the standard Masoretic Text]. Ten of these letters are simply a matter of spelling, which does not affect the [meaning]. Four more letters are minor stylistic changes, such as conjunctions. The remaining three letters comprise the word "light," which is added in verse 11, and does not affect the meaning greatly.[21]

What an encouragement to know that many scholars believe that the Masoretic Text is more accurate than the Isaiah of the Scrolls! That means that the Bible people have loved and read throughout the centuries is based on better texts than the Dead Sea Scrolls turned out to be!

Millar Burrows, in his book *The Dead Sea Scrolls,* writes, "It is a matter of wonder that through something like a thousand years the text underwent so little alteration."[22]

Remember, when scribes transcribed a page they would actually count the number of words and even the letters to make sure that the manuscripts matched each other. Thanks to such standards of accuracy, the Hebrew text of the Old Testament available to scholars today is essentially like that of the original. The Dead Sea Scrolls simply confirmed the overall accuracy of the scribal transmission.

Also, we must point out that a text from one of the scrolls speaks about "a leader of the community being put to death." The text uses terms associated with the Messiah, such as "the staff" and "the Branch of David" and the "Root of Jesse." This shows that although the majority of the Jews in Christ's day awaited a political messiah who would deliver them from

Roman occupation, there were some who believed that the Messiah would suffer and die.[23]

In sum, the Dead Sea Scrolls confirm that what we hold in our hands is a reliable copy of the original documents. We can safely say that the Word of God has been preserved throughout the centuries so that we might know His will for us and His plans for a future world.

I conclude with the words of Millar Burrows: "The general reader and student of the Bible may be satisfied to note that nothing in all this changes our understanding of the religious teaching of the Bible."[24]

BIBLE PROPHECIES PROVE ITS TRUTHFULNESS

Days before Princess Diana was killed, a psychic predicted that she would marry Dodi Al Fayed. This prophetess would have done much better if she had either made an ambiguous prediction that could have been reinterpreted; or even better, made several ambiguous predictions, one of which might be reshaped to fit the facts. No doubt she has long since been forgiven by her clients, who are not troubled by a few wrong predictions. Mystery, not accuracy, is what counts in the psychic business.

Prophecy can be fun. If you can predict the future even once, your friends will respect you and people whom you have never met will stand in awe of your power and influence. But your primary allies are ambiguity, riddles, and contingencies ("if *this* happens . . . then *that* will happen"); such ambiguous statements will enable you to reinterpret a wrong prediction. Your reputation is important, but being clear about what you have said is not.

Enter Nostradamus.

THE PROPHECIES OF NOSTRADAMUS

This famous soothsayer would sometimes put himself in a trance by sitting on a brass tripod with his spine erect; the tripod's legs were placed at the same degree as the pyramids of Egypt. He told us, "I emptied my soul, brain and heart of all care and attained a state of tranquility." Then, staring into a bowl of steaming water as it gave forth its vapors, he recorded his predictions in nearly one thousand quatrains (four lines of verse) that he divided into ten sections. They were written in a mishmash of French, Old Provincial, and Latin.

What intrigues scholars is that he tossed in baffling word games, puns, number codes, and other mysterious anagrams. Then, to confuse things all the more, he deliberately scrambled the order of the verses to disguise their chronology. Although he died in France in 1566, many believe that he predicted events that will engulf the world until the year 8000!

Nostradamus descended from a long line of clairvoyants and early in life believed prophecy would be his destiny. While studying in Avignon, France, he spent his time learning about occultism and astrology. Soon the nobility in France sought him out, demanding his advice and profiting from his uncanny predictions.

How much did Nostradamus know? Some believe he even predicted the rise of Hitler. Let me quote one of his famous prophecies so that you can judge for yourself the degree of his accuracy.

> In the year that is to come soon, and not far from Venus,
> The two greatest ones of Asia and Africa,
> Shall be said to come from the Rhine and Ister,
> Crying and tears shall be at Malta and on the Italian shore.[1]

If you missed seeing Hitler in this prophecy, his followers tell us that the name *Ister* is Hitler. But it is much more likely that *Ister* refers to a river, since another version of the same prophecy says, "From the Rhine and Lower Danube they will be said to have come."

If you're still confused, here is one that the experts tell us predicted the *death* of Hitler.

> He who by iron shall destroy his father, born in Nonnaire,
> Shall in the end carry the blood of the gorgon,
> Shall in a strange country make all so silent,
> That he shall burn himself, and his double talk.[2]

Is it any wonder that scholars disagree among themselves as to how to interpret these lines? Only through ingenious re-interpretations, substitute meanings, and a lively imagination can this prophecy be made to fit.

Read this quatrain and see if you can figure out what twentieth-century events he might have had in mind.

> The great man will be struck down in the day by a thunderbolt,

The evil deed predicted by the bearer of a petition;
According to the prediction another falls at night time.
Conflict in Reims, London, and pestilence at Tuscany.[3]

This, we are told, describes the assassination of President Kennedy and the murder of his brother Robert. Even if we grant that the president was struck down in the day by a "thunderbolt," we are still left wondering who the bearer of the petition might be; and if the one who "falls" is Robert Kennedy, why the references to Reims, London, and "pestilence at Tuscany"?

Other Nostradamus scholars give this quatrain an entirely different interpretation, connecting it with the taking over of Czechoslovakia by Hitler and the dissension between England and France. Perhaps now you can better understand why Nostradamus scholars differ among themselves about virtually every text. Indeed, during World War II Hitler used Nostradamus in his favor; the Allies used the same prophecies as an omen of victory for them.

What can we say about his predictions?

First, many of them are simply too obscure to interpret. For example, only once did he actually specify a date: he made reference to an Antichrist and connected it with the year 1999. Some thought that 1999 was the year Antichrist was to be revealed; other interpreters said that was the year he was to be born. Though the date is specific, exactly what was supposed to have happened is anyone's guess.

Second, we must be generous enough to say that there might be some predictions that did come to pass, or at least some similar events have happened. On a good day, Nostradamus just might have been right about some local events, and he might have had a hunch about some global events too.

If we agree, as I believe we must, that unaided human reason cannot see into the future, we must ask: From where did Nostradamus get his information? According to the Bible there would be only two sources: God or the devil.

That Nostradamus did not get his information from God seems clear for two reasons.

First, he violated the express teaching of God's Word to shun astrology. God warned His people that they should keep away from looking to the stars for guidance. And so this French prophet received information from a source God specifically forbade (see Isaiah 47:12–14).

Second, even his most ardent followers admit that Nostradamus was often wrong. The Scriptures are very clear that if he were wrong but once, he should be condemned as a false prophet. The reason is clear enough: If a prophet receives a revelation from God, he will be right 100 percent of the time. In the Old Testament a false prophet was to be stoned (Deuteronomy 18:20).

Keep in mind that false prophets occasionally predict the future accurately. In the same passage God warns that an accurate, isolated prediction does not in itself prove the validity of the prophet's doctrine.

> If a prophet, or one who foretells by dreams, appears among you and announces to you a sign or wonder, and if the sign or wonder spoken of *takes place,* and the prophet says, "Let us follow other gods" (gods you have not known) "and let us worship them," you must not listen to the words of that prophet or dreamer. . . . That prophet or dreamer must be put to death for inciting rebellion against the Lord your God. (DEUTERONOMY 13:1–3, 5 NIV, emphasis added)

A false prophet might get it right sometimes, but only God gets it right every time. If Nostradamus could see how movie stars and political celebrities are willing to make his prophecies "fit," he would be startled at the attention his garbled prophecies are receiving. He would, I think, marvel at the lengths to which some misguided souls are willing to go to find hidden meanings and allusions to historical events in his writings.

Thankfully, there is a book with prophecies that are so specific, so unambiguous, and so accurate that we must conclude that the writers were inspired by God.

BIBLICAL PROPHECY

Biblical prophecy is not written in riddles and obtuse references. It names places, events, and even people in detail. We might ponder the when, the how, and the why, but we are not left with a half dozen confusing interpretations. Bible prophecy is written in plain language.

If God is God, we can expect His prophets to write about the future with the same assurance as historians write about the past. For God, the future is as the past. "Remember the former things long past, for I am God, and there is no other; ... there is no one like Me, *declaring the end from the beginning, and from ancient times things which have not been done, saying,* 'My purpose will be established, and I will accomplish all My good pleasure'" (Isaiah 46:9–10, emphasis added). Fulfilled prophecy is one more reason to believe that the Bible is of divine origin.

Not surprisingly, God invites us to compare His prophecies with those of other religions (Isaiah 41:21–29). He challenges His people to bring forth the sayings of their seers to find out who is right! Comparisons are in order.

Here are a few examples.

The Prediction about Cyrus, King of Persia

That God reigns in the kingdoms of this world is the consistent teaching of Scripture. Thus God not only knows the future, but also through secondary causes orders it. We should not be surprised that He knows future individuals and nations with unerring accuracy.

How would you like to predict who will be the president of the United States 150 years from now? And, at the same time, describe what will be one of his most important domestic/foreign policy decisions? That is something only God could do.

And in the case of Cyrus, king of Persia, that is exactly what God did! Let's consider some background facts: When Isaiah was writing (700–680 BC) Babylon was just barely coming into its own. He predicted that this nation would eventually surround Jerusalem and take the Jews captive. That prediction was fulfilled about a hundred years later, in three stages, culminating in the siege of 586 BC That prophecy in itself was remarkable.

Not only did Isaiah predict that Babylon would conquer Jerusalem, but he went on to say that the Persians, in turn, would conquer Babylon. Keep in mind that when this prediction was made, Persia was barely in existence. Isaiah predicted that Persia would become a world power and conquer Babylon. That prophecy was also remarkably fulfilled. And then Isaiah added that the king of Persia would allow the captive Jews to return to Jerusalem. It happened just as he said.

Now comes an even more astonishing prediction: Isaiah, speaking for God, *actually names the king who will rule the*

Persian Empire and let the Jews return to Jerusalem! No wonder he repeatedly begins his prophecy with "thus says the Lord." Only the Lord could say what Isaiah does.

Read it carefully.

> It is I who says of Jerusalem, "She shall be inhabited!"
> And of the cities of Judah, "They shall be built." And I
> will raise up her ruins again. . . . It is I who says of *Cyrus*,
> "He is My shepherd! And he will perform all My desire."
> And he declares of Jerusalem, "She will be built," and of
> the temple, "Your foundation will be laid." (ISAIAH 44:26,
> 28, emphasis added)

Cyrus is mentioned as the man who will let the Jews return to their land and rebuild Jerusalem. Isaiah named him and predicted this foreign policy decision more than one hundred years before Cyrus was born!

Isaiah has more to say.

> Thus says the Lord to Cyrus His anointed, whom I have
> taken by the right hand, to subdue nations before him,
> and to loose the loins of kings; to open doors before him
> so that gates will not be shut: . . . "I will give you the trea-
> sures of darkness, and hidden wealth of secret places, so
> that you may know that *it is I, the Lord, the God of Israel,
> who calls you by your name.*" (45:1, 3, emphasis added)

To review the facts: Everyone agrees that the founder of the Persian Empire, Cyrus, ruled over the Persians from 559–530 BC and that during his reign he conquered Babylon in 539 BC Historians tell us that his decree that allowed the Jews to return to their homeland was issued in March 538 BC, just after his capture of Babylon.

Keep in mind that the dates of Isaiah were 700–680 BC. A bit of math tells us that Isaiah named Cyrus and foretold the decision he would make some 100 years before he was born and 150 years before he arose to be king of the land! Jeremiah (626–586 BC) predicted that the captivity of the Jews would be seventy years (Jeremiah 25:11–12; 29:10), and so in accordance with this prophecy, we read in Ezra, "In the first year of Cyrus king of Persia, in order to fulfill the word of the Lord spoken by Jeremiah, the Lord moved the heart of Cyrus king of Persia to make a proclamation throughout his realm and also to put it in writing" (1:1 NIV). Through the decision of Cyrus, both Isaiah's and Jeremiah's prophecies were fulfilled. *Thus God named the king a century and a half in advance and told us that he would issue a decree to release the Jews.*

Why did God make these startling predictions?

First, in Isaiah 44, He contrasts Himself to false prophets whose wisdom He rightly ridicules, "I, the Lord, am the maker of all things, stretching out the heavens by Myself and spreading out the earth all alone, causing the omens of boasters to fail, making fools out of diviners, causing wise men to draw back, and turning their knowledge into foolishness" (Isaiah 44:24–25). The wisdom of the astrologers is brought to shame, but the wisdom of God endures.

Second, God wanted us to stand in awe of all His works. He says He chose Cyrus before he could know his Creator, so that we might better understand the scope of divine authority. "I am the Lord, and there is no other; besides Me there is no God. I will gird you, though you have not known Me; that men may know from the rising to the setting of the sun that there is no one besides Me. I am the Lord, and there is no other" (Isaiah 45:5–6).

God put His own reputation on the line. Of course,

history turned out exactly as God knew it would. There are some predictions only God can make, and this was one of them. Nothing ambiguous here, just prophecy written as clearly as if it were history.

The Prediction about Tyre

Several years ago I visited the ancient city of Tyre, situated in the country of Lebanon. As we walked along a causeway, our guide said, "You are standing where biblical prophecy has been fulfilled." He was right.

Here is the background to the story. Ezekiel prophesied that God would raise up Nebuchadnezzar king of Babylon to come against Tyre with his army of horsemen and that the people would be destroyed. Here is a description of what Tyre would eventually look like when God's judgment was over.

> Therefore this is what the Sovereign Lord says: I am against you, Tyre, and I will bring many nations against you, like the sea casting up its waves. They will destroy the walls of Tyre and pull down her towers; I will scrape away her rubble and make her a bare rock. Out in the sea she will become a place to spread fishnets, for I have spoken, declares the Sovereign Lord. She will become plunder for the nations, and her settlements on the mainland will be ravaged by the sword. Then they will know that I am the Lord. (Ezekiel 26:3–6 NIV)

The prophecy goes on to say that Nebuchadnezzar king of Babylon would come against the city with many horses and will kill the people of Tyre. Then the prophecy repeats:

> They will plunder your wealth and loot your merchandise; they will break down your walls and demolish your

fine houses and throw your stones, timber and rubble into the sea. . . . I will make you a bare rock, and you will become a place to spread fishnets. You will never be rebuilt, for I the Lord have spoken, declares the Sovereign Lord. (26:12, 14 NIV)

Let's review the details of this prophecy:

1. Nebuchadnezzar will destroy the city of Tyre.
2. Many nations would come against Tyre.
3. Tyre will become bare like the top of a flat rock.
4. Fishermen will spread their nets over the site.
5. Tyre will be thrown into the water and never be rebuilt.

All of these predictions were fulfilled by Nebuchadnezzar and Alexander the Great. To understand how this happened, we must keep in mind that Tyre was both a coastal city and an island city. The coastal city of Tyre was besieged by Nebuchadnezzar for thirteen years and destroyed. But many people were able to escape to the island using ships. There, a half-mile from the shore, they built strong fortifications. Nebuchadnezzar, already exhausted with conquering the coastal city, did not bother to take the island.

For 240 years the island city of Tyre survived while its mainland was in ruins. It appeared that Ezekiel's prophecy would not be completely fulfilled, for Tyre was not cast into the sea and "many nations" had not come against her as predicted.

But God had spoken. And one day Alexander the Great marched through the land and was forced to deal with the rebel city of Tyre. After conquering the Persians, he marched down the coast of Palestine until he reached Tyre in 333 BC. Strategically, he knew it was not wise to continue his trek to Egypt leaving the powerful city of Tyre at his rear. The logical step was to conquer the island city with its ships and fortifications.

When he requested the opportunity to enter the city so that he might worship their god Hercules, his request was refused. Evidently the inhabitants knew that Alexander's real motive was to bring soldiers into the city to overtake it. Thus the great Greek general had little choice but to conquer the city in whatever way possible.

The city was well fortified, and Alexander's soldiers could not get near without facing rocks thrown from the high walls. He hit on the idea of building a causeway from the mainland to the island. Although the project went well at first, as the soldiers neared the island, the depth of the water and the harassment increased. *Despite storms and countless attacks, the soldiers of Alexander built the causeway by pushing the ruins of the coastal city into the sea; yes, even the dust was cast into the sea, just as Ezekiel predicted!*

Building the causeway and organizing a navy to conquer the city was not easy. Alexander organized a flotilla of ships from several conquered nations, including 80 from Sidon, Aradus, and Byblos; 10 from Rhodes; 10 from Lycia; and 120 from Cyprus. *As God predicted, many nations came against Tyre!*[4]

Three years after he had begun his siege of Tyre, he conquered the city. Tyre lost eight thousand men in battle, and another two thousand men of military age were crucified around the city; thirty thousand women and children were sold as slaves.

Although there is a small town on the island (the peninsula from Alexander's causeway), the city of Tyre has never been rebuilt. Even today, fishermen spread their nets on the flat rocks of the conquered city, a testimony to the fulfillment of Ezekiel's prophecy. God had said, "I will make you a bare rock, and you will become a place to spread fishnets. You will never be rebuilt, for I the Lord have spoken" (Ezekiel 26:14 NIV). Tyre is on our maps today only because the modern city is in a different location from that of ancient times.

"How unlikely it all was!" wrote Arthur Custance. "What kind of human foresight would have enabled a man to foresee that a thriving city stretching for twenty miles along the shore, of which seven miles were densely populated and built up with large buildings, would one day be desolated and then laid in the midst of the sea, even its very dust? But it all came to pass."[5]

How unlikely! But God had spoken!

The Predictions of Daniel

Daniel was a most remarkable prophet who foresaw the major kingdoms that would arise in the Near East. He predicted the Medo-Persian, Greek, and Roman Empires in such detail that even honest skeptics must admit that he received his visions from God.

In his first vision he saw a statue of a man. The head was gold and represented the nation of Babylon; the breast and arms were silver, representing Medo-Persia; its belly and thighs were bronze, representing Greece; and finally its legs were of iron, representing Rome.

Daniel not only told King Nebuchadnezzar what he had dreamed, but he interpreted it for him:

> You, O king, are the king of kings, to whom the God of heaven has given the kingdom, the power, the strength, and the glory; . . . You are the head of gold. After you there will arise another kingdom inferior to you, then

101

another third kingdom of bronze, which will rule over all the earth. Then there will be a fourth kingdom as strong as iron. (DANIEL 2:37–40)

If there should be any doubt as to the kingdoms predicted, they are actually identified in Daniel 8. The kingdom which would follow Babylon is named Medo-Persia; then follows Greece; and, of course, Rome.

What is most startling is that Daniel gave vivid details of the rise of Alexander the Great and the fact that after his death his kingdom would be divided among four rulers.

> And a mighty king will arise, and he will rule with great authority and do as he pleases. But as soon as he has arisen, his kingdom will be broken up and parceled out toward the four points of the compass, though not to his own descendants, nor according to his authority which he wielded, for his sovereignty will be uprooted and given to others besides them. (11:3–4)

Some two hundred years after Daniel wrote, Alexander, who had no heirs, arose; and after his death his kingdom was divided among his four generals.

What follows in the succeeding passages of Daniel are descriptions of the conflict that would take place between the "king of the South" (the Ptolemies) and the "king of the North" (the Seleucids) (11:5–15). It even speaks of an eventual alliance that will be sealed by a "daughter of the king of the South" (v. 6) who turned out to be Ptolemy II's daughter Berenice. Daniel predicted battle after battle, giving the details of who would do what. As the plot thickened, Daniel wrote as if he had a front-row seat.

He continued by predicting the rise of Antiochus

Epiphanes, who would invade Israel and humiliate the Jews. Listen to this description: "In his place a despicable person will arise, on whom the honor of kingship has not been conferred, but he will come in a time of tranquility and seize the kingdom by intrigue" (v. 21). Daniel spoke of the fact that he would pollute the temple: "Forces from him will arise, desecrate the sanctuary fortress, and do away with the regular sacrifice. And they will set up the abomination of desolation" (v. 31). This, of course, was fulfilled when Antiochus sacrificed a sow on the altar in Jerusalem and thus desecrated the temple. Despite his vile persecutions and apparent victories, he ended in humiliation, just as Daniel predicted.

It has been estimated that there are 135 prophecies in Daniel 11:1–35, all of which were literally fulfilled! Near the end of the chapter, Daniel turned his attention to a future ruler, most probably the Antichrist who is yet to come. Antiochus foreshadows this evil man who "will exalt and magnify himself above every god and will speak monstrous things against the God of gods; and he will prosper until the indignation is finished, for that which is decreed will be done" (v. 36).

Only God could know such details more than two hundred years before the events took place. Only a prophet inspired by God could write prophecy as though it were history!

Messianic Prophecies

God predicted details regarding Christ's first coming so that the identification of the Messiah would be obvious to those who wanted to know the truth. For example, when the wise men came to see Christ, the scribes in Jerusalem were able to tell them that the Christ would be born in Bethlehem (Matthew 2:6, quoting Micah 5:2). And many people understood that the Messiah's coming would be heralded by a special messenger because of what they had read in Isaiah 40:3 and Malachi 3:1 (see Matthew 3:1–2 and Mark 1:2–3, which quote those two Old Testament passages). Dozens of other predictions identified the Messiah.

There is a story that comes to us from the pages of the CIA to illustrate how precise identifications are sometimes made. A Soviet double agent who fled to Mexico was to meet with the secretary of the Russian ambassador in Mexico so that he might receive his passport.

Six prearranged signs were given both to the ambassador and to the spy so there was no possibility of misidentification. When in Mexico City, the spy was (1) to write a letter to the secretary signing his name as "I. Jackson." After three days (2) he was to go to the Plaza de Colon in Mexico City and (3) stand before the statue of Columbus, (4) with his middle finger placed in a guidebook. In addition, when he was approached, (5) he was to say it was a magnificent statue and that he was from Oklahoma and (6) the secretary was then to give him his passport.[6]

If these requirements were met, the odds are that a proper identification would be made. In the case of Christ, there were not six, but dozens of predictions that identified Him as the coming Messiah. To those with an open mind, there need not have been a mistaken identification.

Here is a sampling:

- *His birthplace.* "But as for you, Bethlehem Ephrathah, too little to be among the clans of Judah, from you One will go forth for Me to be ruler in Israel" (Micah 5:2).

THE NEW TESTAMENT FULFILLMENT. When the wise men came from the east to find the Messiah the scribes in Jerusalem knew, on the basis of this prediction, that the Messiah would be born in Bethlehem. Thus seven hundred years before Christ was born his birthplace was foretold.

- *His attitude toward His accusers.* "He was oppressed and He was afflicted, yet He did not open His mouth; like a lamb that is led to the slaughter, and like a sheep that is silent before its shearers" (Isaiah 53:7).

THE NEW TESTAMENT FULFILLMENT. "Then Pilate said to Him, 'Do You not hear how many things they testify against You?' And He did not answer him with regard to even a single charge, so the governor was quite amazed" (Matthew 27:13–14).

- *His burial in a rich man's tomb.* "His grave was assigned with wicked men, yet He was with a rich man in His death, because He had done no violence, nor was there any deceit in His mouth" (Isaiah 53:9).

THE NEW TESTAMENT FULFILLMENT. "When it was evening, there came a rich man from Arimathea, named Joseph, who himself had also become a disciple of Jesus. This man went to Pilate and asked for the body of Jesus. Then Pilate ordered it to be given to him. And Joseph took the body and wrapped it in a clean linen cloth, and laid it in his own new tomb, which he had hewn out in the rock; and he rolled a large stone against the entrance of the tomb and went away" (Matthew 27:57–60).

- *That He would rise from the dead.* "For You will not abandon my soul to Sheol; nor will You allow Your Holy

One to undergo decay" (Psalm 16:10).

THE NEW TESTAMENT FULFILLMENT. In the New Testament Peter quoted this passage, and then showed why it has to apply to Christ and not David: "Brethren, I may confidently say to you regarding the patriarch David that he both died and was buried, and his tomb is with us to this day. And so, because he was a prophet and knew that God had sworn to him with an oath to seat one of his descendants on his throne, he looked ahead and spoke of the resurrection of the Christ, that He was neither abandoned to Hades, nor did His flesh suffer decay" (Acts 2:29–31).

- *That He would be seated at the right hand of God.* "The Lord says to my Lord: 'Sit at My right hand until I make Your enemies a footstool for Your feet'" (Psalm 110:1).

THE NEW TESTAMENT FULFILLMENT. "And after He had said these things, He was lifted up while they were looking on, and a cloud received Him out of their sight" (Acts 1:9). The author of Hebrews confirmed that Christ ascended and that this is further proof that Christ is greater than angels (Hebrews 1:13; cf. vv. 3–4).

Because these predictions have been fulfilled literally we can be confident that other prophecies regarding Christ will also come to pass. The promise given at His ascension is that He would return literally, just as He was taken up into heaven. Listen to His own words: "But immediately after the tribulation of those days the sun will be darkened, and the moon will not give its light, and the stars will fall from the sky, and the powers of the heavens will be shaken. And then the sign of the Son of Man will appear in the sky, and then all the tribes of the earth will mourn, and they will see the Son of Man coming on the clouds of the sky with power and great glory" (Matthew 24:29–30).

The difference between these and Nostradamus are quite evident; there are no riddles, no vague allusions that could be interpreted in a number of different ways. The prophecies are straightforward, specific, and for those who have an open mind, convincing.

Were Prophecy Fulfillments Just Rigged?

Sam Harris suggests it would have been easy for the writers of the New Testament to write their accounts to make them fulfill Old Testament prophecies, as though perhaps in one grand conspiracy to rig the facts: "Wouldn't it have been within the power of any mortal to write a book that confirms the predictions of a previous book?"[7]

Well, first of all, most of Jesus' apostles and the New Testament writers ultimately died for their faith in Him and in His resurrection. They changed from hiding out for fear of discovery to proclaiming the gospel with boldness. It's hard to imagine them doing that for the sake of a made-up story.

> When the disciples wrote their gospel accounts of Christ's life, they were doing so in a hostile environment in which any attempt to be cute with the known facts would be immediately turned against them. It is in this setting that we should take note of the prophecies of Christ's birthplace in Bethlehem (a hard event to stage), the betrayal price that Judas took, the details of Christ's passion, and, most important, the predictions of His resurrection. Coming back from the dead after

three days in the tomb is notoriously hard to rig. As the apostle Paul once put it, "these things were not done in a corner" (Acts 26:26). Everybody was watching what was happening, friend and foe alike. After-the-fact prophecy-fulfillment is not hard in a vacuum, but it would have been hard in the circumstances in which the Christian faith first took root.[8]

Most of Jesus' apostles and the New Testament authors suffered humiliation, torture, and martyrdom for writing and telling people the truth about Him. Why would they endure that if they were just lying about Him?

YOU DECIDE

"There is only one real inevitability: it is necessary that the Scripture be fulfilled," said Carl F. Henry. Christ frequently used the word *must* when referring to His own life and ministry. "I *must* go to Jerusalem. . . . The Scriptures *must* be fulfilled."

The authors of the Bible wrote not merely their own thoughts, but the revelation of God. It is simply not possible for human beings of themselves to have seen so far and so accurately into the future. The biblical prophets did not write riddles; they did not tease us with obscure references that could have a variety of meanings. Unlike some predictions that become clear only after they have happened, these prophecies would have, for the most part, been understandable to those who lived in the prophet's day.

Keep in mind that past fulfillment guarantees future fulfillment. There are still dozens of prophecies in the Bible that will be fulfilled in the future, some perhaps in our lifetime. Peter warned that since Christ has not yet returned, some would become skeptical, mocking the promises of God. "Know this first of all, that in the last days mockers will come with their mocking, following after their own lusts, and saying, 'Where is the promise of His coming? For ever since the fathers fell asleep, all continues just as it was from the beginning of creation'" (2 Peter 3:3–4).

But the same Christ who came in Bethlehem will come to the Mount of Olives (Zechariah 14:1–4) and a line will be drawn between believers and unbelievers. He will separate the "sheep" from the "goats," just as He said.

It is inevitable.

FOR FURTHER CONSIDERATION

Bible Codes

Are there hidden Bible codes that can predict the future?

In the book *The Bible Code,* by Michael Drosnin, the author says that he flew to Israel to meet with a close friend of Yitzhak Rabin in order to warn the prime minister that he might be assassinated. In a letter, Drosnin wrote, "The reason I am warning you about this is that the only time your full name Yitzhak Rabin is encoded in the Bible, the words, 'assassin that will assassinate' cross your name. That should not be ignored. . . . I think you are in real danger, but that danger can be averted."[9]

Can secret codes actually predict such events? And might this intriguing Bible code lead people to conclude that the Bible is the Word of God? Before I answer these questions, a brief explanation of the code will be helpful.

Harold Gans, a senior mathematician with the United States Department of Defense, spent nineteen days close to his computer as it was performing the details of an intricate experiment. Gans is a religious Jew who has a fascination for the Hebrew text, but he never guessed that his expertise in math, statistics, and code breaking would be of help in uncovering one of the most novel and controversial finds within the pages of the Hebrew Bible.

What Gans and other scholars across the ocean, in Jerusalem, were discovering was that the five books of Moses are filled with a system of intricate codes that cannot be explained if the Bible is simply a human book. Indeed, it appeared to these scholars that the only explanation was that it was written by a divine mind.

How were these codes found?

First of all, we must remember that the mathematicians worked only from the original Hebrew text, not a translation. Indeed, Hebrew tradition had always taught that the books of the Law were given to Moses word for word. Thus each letter was important, and hidden meanings, it was believed, were bound to reside in a text so sacred.

Second, these scholars regarded the text as simply a string of letters (spaces were discounted), and they programmed computers to seek for names and words that are spelled in equidistant letter sequences. Every third letter might spell a name going from left to right and, perhaps, a nearby descriptive but related word would be found strung out diagonally, also spelled by using every third letter.

To help explain what they were about, the researchers used this example: If we had a text that was written in a foreign language that we did not understand, it would be very difficult for us to know whether the text was meaningful or meaningless. But if we had a partial dictionary that enabled us to recognize a small number of words, and if we found a pair of conceptually related words, such as *hammer* and *anvil*, in close proximity, we might have reason to think that the text might be meaningful. If we found other pairs in close proximity, such as *chair* and *table*, we might be more convinced that the text was not just a random assortment of letters.

The programmers would suggest various configurations of letters asking the computers to do the collation. If no meanings were found using two letter intervals, they tried three or four. And if not three or four then five or six, all the way up to the hundreds and thousands. Eventually, interesting sequences surfaced.

The scholars built a list of personalities along with the dates of their birth or death by choosing the names from *The Encyclopedia of Great Men in Israel*. They were surprised to discover that the names and dates of their births or deaths were encoded into the text in close proximity. The possibility of sheer coincidence seems well-nigh impossible.

Five mathematical scholars, two from Harvard, two from Hebrew University, and one from Yale, have signed a public statement that reads in part:

> The present work represents serious research carried out by serious investigators. Since the interpretation of the phenomenon in question is enigmatic and controversial, one may want to demand a level of statistical significance beyond what would be demanded for more routine conclusions. . . . The results obtained are sufficiently striking to deserve a wider audience and to encourage further study.[10]

We might grant that there are interesting configurations and pairs of words, but can these codes predict the future? The answer, I strongly believe, is *no*.

Since the Rabin "prediction," if it can be called such, has received much publicity, we will let it serve as an example. The computer found that if you skip every 4,772 letters, the name *Yitzhak Rabin* is embedded in the biblical text. In other words, once the first letter of his name was found, the second letter was found 4,772 letters later, and so on. That means that if you printed out the Pentateuch in rows 4,772 letters wide, the name *Yitzhak Rabin* will appear in the vertical column. But since no piece of paper is wide enough to print out that many letters, Drosnin's book includes a matrix on a standard page, ignoring the many letters and giving the false impression that Rabin's name appears in close proximity on a page of the Bible with the word *assassination* crossing it.

The facts are these. In Hebrew, *Yitzhak Rabin* is eight letters; a letter appears in each of the following passages in Deuteronomy (2:33; 4:42; 7:20; 11:1; 13:11; 17:5; 21:5; and 24:16). Drosnin claims that one of these verses (4:42) has the words "assassin will assassinate" in it. Read the verse and decide for yourself: "Then Moses set apart three cities across the Jordan to the east, that a *manslayer might flee there, who unintentionally slew his neighbor* without having enmity toward him in time past; and by fleeing to one of these cities he might live" (vv. 41–42, emphasis added). The key phrase is translated by Drosnin as "assassin who will assassinate." But it is a mistranslation.[11]

Doron Witztum, who has spent years of research uncovering hidden codes he believes are embedded in the text, thinks that books such as *The Bible Code* will only compromise legitimate research in this area. Even if there *are* codes, they cannot be used to make predictions. First, the Hebrew text we have has spelling changes from the originals; thus researchers cannot be dogmatic about the number of letters.

THE EARTH

This spectacular "blue marble" image is the most detailed true-color image of the entire Earth to date. Using a collection of satellite-based observations, scientists and visualizers stitched together months of observations of the land surface, oceans, sea ice, and clouds into a seamless, true-color mosaic of every square kilometer (.386 square mile) of our planet.

NASA Goddard Space Flight Center Image by Reto Stöckli (land surface, shallow water, clouds). Enhancements by Robert Simmon (ocean color, compositing).
http://visibleearth.nasa.gov/

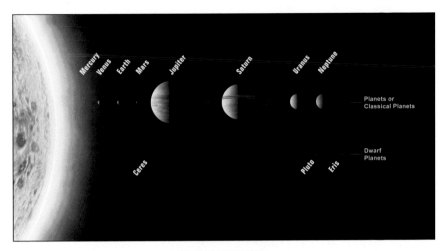

THE SOLAR SYSTEM

This annotated image shows an artist's impression of the solar system.
The International Astronomical Union/Martin Kornmesser

SPIRAL GALAXY M33

More than a billion stars form the whirling spiral galaxy Messier 33 (M33) in the constellation Triangulum. Its spiral arms glow blue with the light of hot, new stars. Older, yellow stars populate the nucleus. At a distance of only 3.5 billion light-years, M33 is one of the nearest spiral galaxies.

Tom Montemayor/McDonald Observatory

Qumran community buildings cistern
Courtesy of Israel Ministry of Tourism

Qumran and the Dead Sea from the west
David Biven/LifeintheHolyLand.com

Qumran cave 4
Courtesy of Israel Ministry of Tourism

Qumran cave 4 interior
Todd Bolen/BiblePlaces.com

Qumran from the west with marl terraces and caves
Todd Bolen/BiblePlaces.com

Qumran looking south: the Dead Sea Scrolls were written here and found nearby.
Courtesy of Israel Ministry of Tourism

Isaiah Scroll
Photo copyright The Israel Museum, Jerusalem

Section from the temple scroll
Photo copyright The Israel Museum, Jerusalem

OVERVIEW OF THE BIBLE

THE OLD TESTAMENT: 39 BOOKS	
Genesis through Deuteronomy	Law
Joshua through Esther	History
Job through Song of Solomon	Poetry and Proverbs
Isaiah through Daniel	Major Prophets
Hosea through Malachi	Minor Prophets
Christ's Redemptive Work Promised (Hebrews 1:1)	

THE NEW TESTAMENT: 27 BOOKS	
Matthew, Mark, Luke, John	Gospels
Book of Acts	Church History
Romans through Thessalonians	Church Epistles
Timothy through Philemon	Pastoral/Individual Epistles
Hebrews through Jude	General Epistles
Book of Revelation	Future Events
Christ's Redemptive Work Fulfilled (Hebrews 1:2–4)	

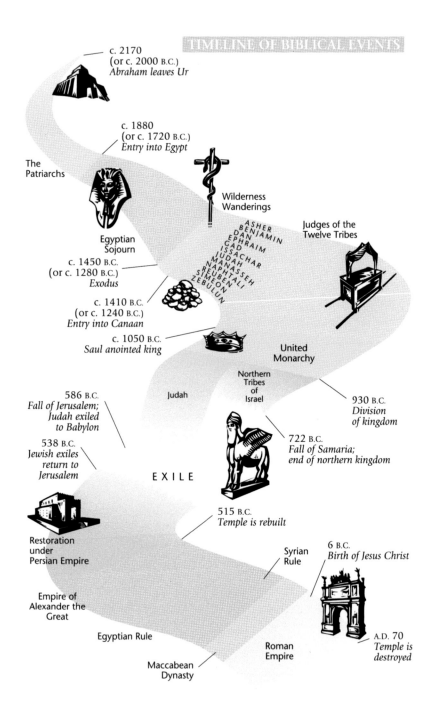

c. 2170
(or c. 2000 B.C.)
Abraham leaves Ur

c. 1880
(or c. 1720 B.C.)
Entry into Egypt

The
Patriarchs

Wilderness
Wanderings

Egyptian
Sojourn

Judges of the
Twelve Tribes

ASHER
BENJAMIN
DAN
EPHRAIM
GAD
ISSACHAR
JUDAH
MANASSEH
NAPHTALI
REUBEN
SIMEON
ZEBULUN

c. 1450 B.C.
(or c. 1280 B.C.)
Exodus

c. 1410 B.C.
(or c. 1240 B.C.)
Entry into Canaan

c. 1050 B.C.
Saul anointed king

United
Monarchy

586 B.C.
*Fall of Jerusalem;
Judah exiled
to Babylon*

Judah

Northern
Tribes
of
Israel

930 B.C.
*Division
of kingdom*

538 B.C.
*Jewish exiles
return to
Jerusalem*

722 B.C.
*Fall of Samaria;
end of northern kingdom*

EXILE

515 B.C.
Temple is rebuilt

Restoration
under
Persian Empire

Syrian
Rule

6 B.C.
Birth of Jesus Christ

Empire of
Alexander the
Great

Egyptian Rule

Roman
Empire

A.D. 70
*Temple is
destroyed*

Maccabean
Dynasty

Copyright © 1996 Tyndale House Publishers, Inc.

Second, Witztum claims that just as there is a code saying that Rabin will be assassinated, so he found a code that Churchill will be assassinated!

Another reason that codes cannot predict the future is that researchers don't know what combinations of words (should they occur) have significance. There are many words that are near each other that have no apparent meaning in relationship to each other. Nevertheless, Witztum believes that there are too many sequences to be explained by chance, though more research is needed to make the enterprise thoroughly scientific. But no predictions can be made on the basis of these discoveries.

These secret codes, though interesting, are fraught with additional dangers. One is that they can draw attention away from the actual message of the Bible. In times past, you had to be a man or woman of God to interpret the Bible; today you just need to be a mathematician and a computer whiz.

Interestingly, physicist and author Randy Ingermanson developed a series of statistical computer tests to probe whether a superintelligent author encoded a large amount of information in the Hebrew Bible text and concluded that the amount of encoded information is either zero or very small.[12]

It is unthinkable that God would hide secret messages in the Bible that could not be discovered until the advent of computers. What He has revealed is necessary for His people throughout all generations. This generation, perhaps as no other, has ignored the plain message of the Bible; we are hardly candidates for more "secret" information.

Finally, will these codes cause people to believe in the Bible and therefore believe in God and His Son? I think not. Proof is that Drosnin himself, the author of *The Bible Code*, said in an interview on CNN, "I am Jewish. But I am not at all religious, and *I don't believe in God.*"[13]

So there you have it. Fascination with the mathematical symmetry of the Bible does not lead people to acceptance of it as the Word of God. The moral and spiritual demands the Bible makes upon those who actually believe it are contrary to prideful human nature and its accomplishments. That's why many who study it are not transformed by its power. Remember, those who are most convinced that the Bible is God's Word are those who are willing to submit to its authority.

"At that time Jesus said, 'I praise You, Father, Lord of heaven and earth, that You have hidden these things from the wise and intelligent and have revealed them to infants'" (Matthew 11:25).

Better to probe and believe the prophecies that are clear, than to seek after those that are obscure. The clearest message we shall ever hear comes through the lips of Christ, and it is to a discussion of His authority that we now turn.

CHRIST AFFIRMED THE BIBLE'S AUTHORITY AND TRUTH

Whenever I see a picture of Jesus on the cover of *Time* or *Newsweek*, I pick up the magazine with misgivings. I know that He will be dissected, analyzed, and stripped of His deity. In the end we will learn about a Jesus who is not qualified to be our Savior, much less worthy of our worship. The man from Nazareth will be putty in the hands of scholars, bent on fashioning Him according to their preference and liking. He will be a no-frills Jesus, reduced to a mere man. He will be an object of fascination, but not adoration.

Do you find your faith shaken when you read that the very existence of Christ is questionable? For example,

Stephen Mitchell, in his book *The Gospel According to Jesus*, wrote, "We can't be sure of anything Jesus actually said."[1] Indeed, *Time* quotes German scholar Rudolf Bultmann as saying that the Gospel accounts are so unreliable that "we can now know almost nothing concerning the life and personality of Jesus."[2]

Why these conclusions?

THE JESUS SEMINAR

You have heard of the Jesus Seminar, a group of scholars who met in California to vote on what they believe Christ did or did not say and do. They devised a creative plan on how to cast their ballots: Each participant drops a plastic bead into a bucket, and the color of the bead signifies the scholar's opinion: *Red* means, "That's Jesus!" *Pink,* "Sure sounds like Jesus"; *Gray,* "Well, maybe"; *Black,* "There has been some mistake."

Their conclusion is that only about 18 percent of the words ascribed to Jesus in the Gospels may have actually been spoken by Him. To no one's surprise, the resurrection of Christ was blackballed, along with all of the other miracles. Only politically correct words and deeds survive.

These left-wing scholars' stated purpose is to change the way people think about Jesus. They have gone public, and national newspapers regularly report their conclusions. They want to "free the Bible from the religious right" and believe that our culture needs a new view of Jesus, a Jesus that speaks to modern concerns such as feminism, multiculturalism, ecology, and political correctness. This is a Jesus according to the spirit of our age.

Bible believers have nothing to fear from these subjective speculations. In fact, properly understood, these scholars actually strengthen our faith rather than undermine it! *Indeed, the Jesus Seminar is just one more reason to believe that Christ is who the New Testament writers claim He is!*

Let me explain.

First, keep in mind that these radical views are entirely based on the subjective hunches of each scholar; in effect, every decision is made with an unwavering bias against miracles. To quote the exact words of the introduction of *The Five Gospels*, a book published by the Jesus Seminar, "The Christ of creed and dogma, who had been firmly in place in the Middle Ages, can no longer command the assent of those who have seen the heavens through Galileo's telescope."[3]

We have seen the heavens, the argument goes, so we can no longer believe in a miraculous Christ. Remember: The "discoveries" are neither historical nor archaeological. Yes, the scholars have extensively studied the life and times of Jesus, but only to try to shape their personal view of who Jesus really was—Jesus the man, the *mere* man.

Keep in mind that for centuries liberal scholars have tried to separate the historical Jesus (Jesus the mere man) from what they call "the Christ of faith," that is, the Christ of legend and myth. They have tried to peel away all of the miraculous sayings and works in the Gospels to find this man, Jesus. But many modern scholars admit that this enterprise has been a gigantic failure. They have ended up with as many different "historical Jesuses" as there are scholars. Rather than writing a biography of Christ, each scholar has, in effect, written a biography of himself! The life of Christ is a mirror in which each scholar sees his own reflection, his own doubts, aspirations, and agenda.

The search for the historical Jesus has been a kind of Rorschach inkblot test. Since these scholars rejected the manuscripts of the New Testament as authoritative and their own conceptions of Jesus were all that mattered, many different portraits of Christ emerged. Some writers pictured Him as a countercultural hippie; others as a Jewish reactionary, a charismatic rabbi, or even a homosexual magician. The famed humanitarian Albert Schweitzer wrote his own biography of Christ and concluded that it was His insanity that drove Him to claim divinity.

In the end, we knew more about the authors of these biographies than we did about Jesus! Their dizzy contradictions and subjective opinions led many scholars to throw up their hands in exasperation and admit that the quest for the historical Jesus has ended in failure. The scholars discovered that the portrait of Christ in the New Testament was a whole piece of cloth; they were not able to find the seam in the garment that would separate "the historical Jesus" from the Christ of faith. No razor blade was sharp enough to carve up the New Testament with any objectivity. Realizing that the search for the historical Jesus was futile, many concluded that the best course of action is simply to say that we know nothing whatever about Him.

In my book *Christ Among Other gods,* I tell the story of the celebrated painting by Burne-Jones named *Love Among Ruins* that was destroyed by an art firm hired to restore it. Although they had been warned that it was a watercolor and therefore needed special attention, the company used the wrong liquid and dissolved the paint.[4]

Throughout the ages men have tried to reduce the bright New Testament portrait of Christ to gray tints, to sponge out the miracles, to humanize His claims. So far, however, no one has found the solvent needed to neutralize the original and reduce it to a cold, dull canvas. No matter who tries to blend its hues with those of ordinary men, the portrait remains intact, immune to those who seek to distinguish between the original and a supposed later addition.

Try as they might, people have not been able to find a purely human Jesus anywhere on the pages of the New Testament. Their subjectivism has left them with random bits and pieces that do not easily fit together. They are faced with a clear choice: *accept Him as portrayed in the New Testament or confess ignorance about Him.* In effect, they are faced with the realization that the gospel portrait is either all true or all false. Determined not to accept a miraculous Christ, they have opted for saying that there might not have been a historical Jesus at all!

Augustine lived before scholars chewed up the Scriptures according to their personal whims. Nevertheless, even in his day, some people believed what they wanted and discarded the rest. He wrote, "If you believe what you like in the gospels, and reject what you don't like, it's not the gospel you believe, but yourself."

Yes!

BELIEVING WHAT JESUS BELIEVED

If we are willing to treat the New Testament with the same respect given to other ancient documents, we discover that they are reliable eyewitness accounts of the life and ministry of Christ. They confront us with a Christ who claimed to be God and had the credentials to prove it.

Here we come to another reason why we believe the Bible is God's Word: *Christ's authority.* Surely His opinion is important, not just for Christians, but even for those who follow Him from a distance. So the question before us is: What was

His opinion of His Bible, the Old Testament?

By appealing to the authority of Christ in establishing the credibility of the Old Testament, we are not reasoning in a circle: The life, death, resurrection, and claims of Christ can be established on independent historical grounds as shown in the last chapter.

One critical scholar said that we cannot know that the Bible is without error because "only an omniscient being" could know that it was accurate in every detail. In Christ, this doubter gets exactly what he wants: *the omniscient Lord, teaching that the Old Testament is without error!*

Christ Believed Old Testament History

We've already learned that Bible critics have written off many of the stories of the Old Testament as mythological. They might talk piously about taking the Bible "seriously" but not "literally"; for all practical purposes what that means is that Adam and Eve did not exist; neither did Noah, Moses, and Jonah, to name a few. No miracles. No personal words from God.

Yet, interestingly, Christ lent His authority to the Old Testament accounts and the miracles associated with them!

Here are just a few examples.

- Adam and Eve are thought by some to be mythological figures, but Christ confirmed the Genesis story: "Have you not read that He who created them from the beginning made them male and female, and said, 'For this reason a man shall leave his father and mother and be joined to his wife, and the two shall become one flesh'?" (Matthew 19:4–5).

• Many people have discounted the story of the flood, but Christ said: "For the coming of the Son of Man will be just like the days of Noah. For as in those days before the flood they were eating and drinking, marrying and giving in marriage, until the day that Noah entered the ark, and they did not understand until the flood came and took them all away; so will the coming of the Son of Man be" (Matthew 24:37–39).

Interestingly, He introduced this affirmation of Noah and the flood with the words, "Heaven and earth will pass away, but My words will not pass away" (Matthew 24:35). Thus we are confronted with a decision: Do we believe those critics who cannot accept the reliability of the story, or do we believe Christ? No wonder liberal critics would prefer to say that we know nothing about the Jesus of history!

But might Christ have simply been using the prevailing belief in a flood to make a point? It has been suggested that He did not believe in the flood Himself, but merely took advantage of contemporary beliefs. But such a conclusion will not do.

In his book *Christ and the Bible*, John Wenham shows that such a view is quite impossible. "The future Judge is speaking words of solemn warning to those who shall hereafter stand convicted at his bar. . . . And yet we are to suppose him to say that an imaginary person who at the imaginary preaching of an imaginary prophet repented in imagination, shall rise up in that day and condemn the actual impenitence of those his actual hearers."[5] Christ believed in the story of Noah and the flood. Do we know better than He?

- We've learned that many scholars do not believe Moses existed because there is no independent confirmation of his life and the story of the Exodus. Christ, however, believed in the account of Moses and God's daily provision of manna. "Our fathers ate the manna in the wilderness; as it is written, 'He gave them bread out of heaven to eat.' Jesus then said to them, 'Truly, truly, I say to you, it is not Moses who has given you the bread out of heaven, but it is My Father who gives you the true bread out of heaven'" (John 6:31–32).

- Christ confirms the two stories often disbelieved in the book of Jonah, namely, that he was swallowed by a fish and that a great revival took place in Nineveh as a result of his preaching. Listen to how Christ understood these events. "An evil and adulterous generation craves for a sign; and yet no sign will be given to it but the sign of Jonah the prophet; for just as Jonah was three days and three nights in the belly of the sea monster, so will the Son of Man be three days and three nights in the heart of the earth. The men of Nineveh will stand up with this generation at the judgment, and will condemn it because they repented at the preaching of Jonah; and behold, something greater than Jonah is here" (Matthew 12:39–41).

Do you doubt that God judged Sodom and Gomorrah for their sin? Or that Lot's wife looked back and became a pillar of salt? Christ consistently referred to such Old Testament accounts as matters of fact. Thus historical happenings in the past are used as a foundation for future expectations.

Later in this book we will show that Christ accepted the

whole scope of Old Testament history from beginning to end. Surely this should give us confidence that the historicity of the Old Testament is to be believed.

Christ Accepted the Authority of the Old Testament

Christ quoted the Old Testament to settle disputes. Yes, there were liberals in His day too. When the Sadducees tried to ridicule the doctrine of the resurrection, He replied, "Is this not the reason you are mistaken, that you do not understand the Scriptures or the power of God?" (Mark 12:24).

He continued, "But regarding the fact that the dead rise again, have you not read in the book of Moses, in the passage about the burning bush, how God spoke to him, saying, 'I am the God of Abraham, and the God of Isaac, and the God of Jacob'? He is not the God of the dead, but of the living; you are greatly mistaken" (vv. 26–27). Christ argued for the resurrection on the basis of one word, a present tense verb! If there were no resurrection, God would have said, "I *was* the God of Abraham," but because God used the present tense, "I *am* the God of Abraham," this must mean that Abraham, Isaac, and Jacob were still alive and would rise again!

The mistake of the Pharisees was not that they had studied the Scriptures too much, but that they had not pondered them sufficiently. Their mistake was not that they applied the law too rigorously, but that they did not probe its deeper meaning (Matthew 23:23). Indeed, Christ pointed out, "Do not think that I have come to abolish the Law or the Prophets; I have not come to abolish them but to fulfill them" (Matthew 5:17 NIV). They were to obey not just the letter, but also the spirit of the Law.

Far from discrediting the Old Testament Scriptures, Christ said, "The scribes and the Pharisees sit on Moses' seat; so practice and observe whatever they tell you, but not what they do; for they preach, but do not practice" (Matthew 23:2–3 RSV). He honored what they taught, again grieved that they understood their teaching so superficially. He chided them for allowing their spiritual blindness and traditions to obscure the meaning of the Law. He said they studied the Scriptures in vain (John 5:39–47).

Christ Approved Old Testament Conduct

Have you ever heard that the Old Testament is irrelevant as a guide to conduct and spiritual values? Christ didn't think so. When a lawyer asked the question, "Which is the great commandment in the Law?" (Matthew 22:36), Christ answered by linking together two quotations from the Old Testament. "'You shall love the Lord your God with all your heart, and with all your soul, and with all your mind.' This is the great and foremost commandment. The second is like it, 'You shall love your neighbor as yourself.'" Then He added, "On these two commandments depend the whole Law and the Prophets" (Matthew 22:37–40).

These are not New Testament commandments, but Old Testament; they lie at the heart of Old Testament Law. Far from the New Testament being disconnected from the Old, it is the fulfillment of it. Any notion that the Old Testament God was a God of wrath and the New Testament is a God of compassion, is unfounded.

Again, a critic might ask: Might it be that Jesus really did not believe in the authority of the Old Testament, but answered His critics on their own ground without pausing to correct their mistaken premises? Thus, Christ, it is said, was more interested in discrediting His opponents than in revealing the foundation of eternal truth.

But elsewhere Christ was not shy about correcting misconceptions. He was not slow to denounce the Pharisees' traditionalism and correct their nationalistic view of the coming Messiah. As Wenham says, "Surely he would have been prepared to explain clearly the mingling of the divine truth and human error in the Bible, if he had known such to exist."[6] It simply does not wash to assume that Christ was aware that the Jews' view of Scripture was wrong but went along with their beliefs anyway, hoping to correct them in some other way.

Keep in mind how Christ faced temptation. Three times He said to Satan, "It is written," then quoted a relevant text from the Old Testament. Obviously, Christ would not have confronted the devil on false premises.

The expression "It is written" in the present tense is better translated, "It *stands* written," which is equivalent to saying, "God says." "Here is the permanent, unchangeable witness of the Eternal God, committed to writing for our use and instruction."[7] As Christ was dying, the Scriptures were on His lips. "My God, My God, why have You forsaken Me?" (Matthew 27:46; cf. Psalm 22:1) and "Into Your hands I commit My spirit" (Luke 23:46; cf. Psalm 31:5).

After the resurrection, He again pointed His disciples to the Scriptures. To those walking on the road to Emmaus, we read, "Then beginning with Moses and with all the prophets, He explained to them the things concerning Himself in all the Scriptures" (Luke 24:27). The Old Testament was characterized by a "God-givenness"; it has the particular distinction of being the Book of God. To say, "The Scripture says," is to say, "God says."

Christ Affirmed Old Testament Prophecies

In chapter 3, I observed that Christ often used the little word *must*, or its equivalent. He used it most often in relationship to Old Testament prophecies. There was no doubt in His mind that the Old Testament Scripture *had* to be fulfilled.

He predicted His death.

- "Behold, we are going up to Jerusalem, and all things which are written through the prophets about the Son of Man *will be* accomplished. For He *will be* handed over to the Gentiles, and *will be* mocked and mistreated and spit upon, and after they have scourged Him, they *will* kill Him; and the third day He *will* rise again" (Luke 18:31–33, emphasis added).
- "For I tell you that this which is written *must* be fulfilled in Me, 'And He was numbered with transgressors'; for that which refers to Me has its fulfillment" (Luke 22:37, emphasis added).
- "The Son of man goes *as it is written* of him" (Matthew 26:24 RSV; Mark 14:21 RSV, emphasis added).
- "Do you think that I cannot appeal to my Father, and he will at once send me more than twelve legions of angels? *But how then should the scriptures be fulfilled, that it must be so?* . . . But all this has taken place, that the scriptures of the prophets might be fulfilled" (Matthew 26:53–54, 56 RSV, emphasis added).
- "O foolish men, and slow of heart to believe all that the prophets have spoken! Was it not *necessary* that the Christ should suffer these things and enter into his glory?" (Luke 24:25–26 RSV, emphasis added).
- "*Thus it is written,* that the Christ should suffer and on the third day rise from the dead, and that repentance and

forgiveness of sins should be preached in his name to all nations, beginning from Jerusalem" (Luke 24:46–47 RSV, emphasis added).

- *"The scriptures*... bear witness to me.... If you believed Moses, you would believe me, for he wrote of me. But if you do not believe his writings, how will you believe my words?" (John 5:39, 46–47 RSV, emphasis added).

- "I am not speaking of you all; I know whom I have chosen; *it is that the scripture may be fulfilled,* 'He who ate my bread has lifted his heel against me'" (John 13:18 RSV, emphasis added; cf. Psalm 41:9).

For Christ, the words of Scripture were God's words. For Him to say, "Have you not read?" is equivalent to saying, "Do you not know that God has said?" He used the phrase *the Word of God* and the word *Scripture* interchangeably when He quoted the Old Testament. For example, the Old Testament reads, "For this reason a man shall leave his father and his mother" (Genesis 2:24). When Christ quoted this verse He did not say, "The Scripture says . . ." Rather, He attributed the words directly to God. *"He who created them . . .* said" (Matthew 19:4–5, emphasis added).

To quote Wenham once more, "Jesus never exalts the Scriptures for their own sake, yet He never allows a wedge to be driven between the Scriptures and the message of Scripture. What Scripture says is the word of God—God is its author."[8]

Christ Affirmed the Inerrancy of the Old Testament

That Christ considered the Old Testament to be authoritative is clear enough, but did He believe that the very words were inspired? "Do not think that I came to abolish the Law or the Prophets; I did not come to abolish, but to fulfill. For truly I say to you, until heaven and earth pass away, not the smallest letter or stroke shall pass from the Law until all is accomplished" (Matthew 5:17–18).

He believed that the accuracy of the Old Testament extended to the smallest letter, which would be equivalent to the dot above the *i* and the stroke that turns a *P* into an *R*. These details are important because letters make up words, and words convey meanings.

Picture Jesus with a group of angry Jews standing around, accusing Him of blasphemy because He claimed to be God. He defended Himself brilliantly by asking, "Is it not written in your law, 'I said, you are gods'?" (John 10:34 RSV). Jesus appealed to the Law because He knew that they would accept its authority. Usually we think the word *Law* refers to the five books of Moses, but in the broader context the law is the entire Old Testament. Christ was actually quoting from Psalm 82:6.

In this very psalm, God is spoken of as the true Judge (vv. 1, 8), but those men who were representing Him were not rendering wise verdicts for God. The word *gods* in verse 1 refers to these human judges. Of course they were not actually "gods," but they did have an important position among men. Just as in the Canadian Parliament there is the house of "lords," though no one would believe for a moment that these men are "Lords" in any divine sense.

Now—and here comes the argument—Christ said that if, in certain situations men could be called "gods," why should He be accused of blasphemy if He called Himself God? After all, His credentials were much more impressive than theirs! Needless to say, His accusers were disarmed.

In this context Christ made an offhand comment that

showed His high regard for the Old Testament. Let's quote the entire verse, "Has it not been written in your Law, 'I said, you are gods'? If he called them gods, to whom the word of God came (*and the Scripture cannot be broken*), do you say of Him, whom the Father sanctified and sent into the world, 'You are blaspheming,' because I said, 'I am the Son of God'?" (John 10:34–36, emphasis added).

Notice how casually Christ let the words "the Scripture cannot be broken" come from His lips. He did not simply mean that this particular Scripture cannot be broken, but simply, "the Scripture cannot be broken," a reference to the Old Testament as a whole. Even in minute particulars this body of literature is accurate.

We've learned that inspiration, if it means anything at all, must extend to the very words of Scripture. The modern notion that the thoughts are inspired, but not the words, misunderstands the nature of language. Of course the Bible represents God's thoughts, but these thoughts were communicated in words, and thus the exact sentences were under the supervision of God. Whether we can accept it or not, Christ believed the Old Testament to the letter.

Suppose you signed a contract with a man who promises to build a house for you. A few days later he wants to deviate from the agreement. You point to the paragraph that specifies what you agreed on, but he replies, "You can't go by the actual words, just the *thoughts* are binding!" Whoa!

Is the Bible pure and free from error? We must ask whether God Himself is pure and free from error. Christ would never have put His approval upon erroneous statements and teachings. We cannot circumvent the plain fact that Christ believed that the Old Testament words were inspired. For Him, *if the Old Testament said it, God said it!*

LIFE-TRANSFORMING APPLICATIONS

"If you don't agree with everything David *did,* then why do you agree with everything he *wrote?*" a liberal pastor said to me as we were discussing the question of original sin. I had defended the doctrine by quoting David in Psalm 51, "In sin did my mother conceive me" (v. 5 RSV). His point was clear: Since David was a fallible man, he could not have written an infallible psalm. Or at least, there is no reason to think he did.

I didn't have an answer for him at the time, but now I do. Christ knew that the authors of the Bible were fallible men, but He affirmed that what they wrote was *in*fallible. It had to be that way if God were to use men to give us the Scriptures.

Christ understood that a man may write what is inspired, and hence true, even if in his personal life, he was fallible. He knew that David, the author of the psalms, was fallible, but what He wrote under divine inspiration was the very word of God. As we have seen, Christ did not make a division between truth and error. He had no need to separate the chaff from the wheat, the false from the true. David wrote under the inspiration of God.

If Christ believed the Old Testament, which included Psalm 51, can we do any less? Do we know more than He about God, science, and history? Let us not be ashamed to say, "The Bible says," for what the Bible says, God says.

A mathematician might try to prove that he can dodge an avalanche because the trajectory of each boulder can be calculated, and that an agile man can step out of the way of any one of the individual rocks. Just so, taken one at a time, a scholar can try to explain away each of Christ's affirmations of the Old Testament. But the statements do not come one at a time, but "form a great avalanche of items of cumulative evidence which cannot in honesty be evaded."[9] We cannot deny that Christ believed in the complete authority of the Old Testament. If He is our Savior, He is also our teacher, and all who accept Him as a teacher must, if they are honest, bow before Him as Savior.

The high priest questioned Christ, but until that moment He had kept silent.

"Are You the Christ, the Son of the Blessed One?"

"I am; and you shall see the Son of Man sitting at the right hand of Power, and coming with the clouds of heaven" (Mark 14:61–62). Those who do not accept Christ as Savior now will meet Him as judge in the future. Either way, a confrontation with Christ is inevitable. The wise will believe what He believed and follow where He leads.

FOR FURTHER CONSIDERATION

Could the Disciples Have Invented the Stories about Jesus?

In the back of our minds, we might be wondering: "Could the disciples have made up the story of Christ? Could the Jesus Seminar have a point when it concludes that a man named Jesus existed and the disciples turned him into the Christ, the Messiah?" Even if we cannot separate the Jesus of history from the Christ of faith, even if we cannot find the "historical Jesus"—still is it possible that His followers were overcome with "messianic fever" and therefore embellished the stories of Christ? Were they capable of turning an ordinary man into a Messiah?

No, either intentionally or unintentionally, the disciples could not have invented Jesus. In *History and Christianity,* Dr. John Warwick Montgomery gives three powerful reasons why the disciples were incapable of taking Jesus the man and making Him into a Messiah of their liking.[10]

First, Jesus, as He is described in the New Testament, differs radically from the kind of Messiah that was anticipated by the Jews of His era. In other words, Jesus was a poor candidate to be "deified."

The late Jewish scholar Edersheim of Oxford University has shown that it was incredible for Christ to proclaim that His desire was not to make Gentiles convert to Judaism but to make *both* Jews and Gentiles "children of one heavenly Father," and not to put the law on the heathen, but rather to deliver Jews and Gentiles from it and "fulfill its demands for all!"

To quote Edersheim, "The most unexpected and unprepared-for revelation was, from the Jewish point of view, that of the breaking down of the middle wall of partition between Jew and Gentile, the taking away of the enmity of the law, and the nailing it to His cross. There was nothing analogous to it. . . . Assuredly, the most unlike thing to Christ were His times."[11] The Jews of the day expected the Messiah to appear with a sword to break the Roman occupation from the land. Some thought He would bring back the remnant of the ten lost tribes and reunite Israel and Judah.

Christ was a bitter disappointment on all counts. The Jews were not about to accept a Messiah who said, "My kingdom is not of this world" (John 18:36). No wonder the Jewish officials arranged His crucifixion. *If the disciples had wanted to choose a man to make into a Messiah, Jesus would not have made the list.*

Second, the disciples were psychologically incapable of taking a man and calling him *God*. The central tenet of Judaism is "Hear, O Israel: The Lord our God is one Lord"

(Deuteronomy 6:4 RSV). The greatest blasphemy was idolatry, that is, calling a person or thing, *God*. For the disciples to deify a mere man would be contradicting the most basic point of the Law, "You shall have no other gods before Me" (Exodus 20:3).

To break such a commandment would mean that they were, in Montgomery's words, either "charlatans or psychotics." He continues: "Yet the picture of them in the documents is one of practical, ordinary, down-to-earth fishermen, hardheaded tax gatherers etc., and people with perhaps more than the usual dose of skepticism."[12]

The point is that the disciples had to be convinced that Christ was the Messiah; there was no way they would have taken a mere man and made him into God.

Third, it was the resurrection that transformed these men into convinced followers of Christ. Read the New Testament accounts and you will discover that they leave no doubt that the writers understood the difference between fact and fiction. They were well aware that false messiahs had come and gone, and thus they were skeptical about Christ. But after He was raised from the dead, they were convinced that Christ was indeed the Messiah, the Savior of the world.

"Doubting Thomas," as the disciple is frequently called, reminds us that Christ is accommodating to skeptics whose hearts are open to embrace the truth but who sincerely believe that there is not enough evidence. Doubt, someone has said, "is stumbling over a stone we do not understand." It has been said that those who have never doubted, have never really believed.

Thomas had a streak of pessimism, a hunch that in the end nothing would ever come out just right. After the resurrection, Christ appeared to His disciples, but Thomas was absent. He was not the kind of disciple who was so gripped with "messianic fever" that he was seeking for a reason to make Christ into a God.

"The other disciples were saying to him, 'We have seen the Lord!' But he said to them, 'Unless I see in His hands the imprint of the nails, and put my finger into the place of the nails, and put my hand into His side, I will not believe'" (John 20:25).

Eight days later, Christ gave Thomas a challenge. "'Reach here with your finger, and see My hands; and reach here your hand and put it into My side; and do not be unbelieving, but believing.' Thomas answered and said to Him, 'My Lord and my God!'" (vv. 27–28).

Christ added, "Because you have seen Me, have you believed? Blessed are they who did not see, and yet believed" (v. 29).

Scripture includes multiple reports in the Gospels and in Paul's letters of Jesus appearing after His death to many witnesses. Still, evidence for Jesus' resurrection does not convince Prof. Richard Dawkins: "Presumably what happened to Jesus was what happens to all of us when we die. We decompose. Accounts of Jesus' resurrection and ascension are about as well-documented as Jack and the Beanstalk."[13]

Dawkins insists, "There is no good historical evidence that [Jesus] ever thought he was divine." Regarding C. S. Lewis's explanation that in claiming to be the Son of God Jesus was either right, insane, or a liar, Dawkins offers "a fourth possibility, almost too obvious to need mentioning . . . that Jesus was honestly mistaken."[14] Yet how can one be simply "mistaken" about thinking one is God? How could anyone think Jesus, who comes across as wise, humble, loving, truthful, and supremely self-sacrificing in the Scriptures, was insane, lying, or "honestly mistaken"?

C. S. Lewis regarded Jesus' teachings as the highest standard of morality known to man, and that creates a big problem for some, the problem of cosmic authority, according to Regis Nicoll: "If Jesus was right about his divinity, then man is not a morally autonomous happenstance, he's a special creation, a being that will one day stand before his Creator." Nicoll quotes one self-described atheist as saying, "It isn't just that I don't believe in God . . . I *hope* there is no God" (emphasis added).[15]

Bruce E. Hunsberger and Bob Altemeyer, who describe themselves as agnostics, have done extensive research among atheists in Canada and the United States and documented their findings in a book.

They found consistent dogmatism in atheists' thinking: "Nearly all of them said that scientifically validated evidence confirming the Gospel accounts of Jesus' public life, death, and resurrection *would have no effect at all* on their beliefs about his divinity. And most said nothing conceivable could lead them to believe in the traditional God" (emphasis added).[16]

On the other hand, German theologian Wolfhart Pannenberg, who does not hold to biblical inerrancy, defends Jesus' resurrection on purely historical grounds.[17] He says, "The evidence for Jesus' resurrection is so strong that nobody would question it except for two things. First, it is a very unusual event. And second, if you believe it happened, you have to change the way you live."[18]

So something other than skepticism about evidence may be the issue for many atheists' unbelief. There's great risk in continually rejecting the truth about God and Jesus Christ. Jesus said to the scribes and Pharisees who refused to believe

Him, "Because I speak the truth, you do not believe me" (John 8:45.) The risk is having God say to you, in effect, "Then believe the lie and be condemned for all eternity." That's what Scripture says:

> The coming of the lawless one is by the activity of Satan with all power and false signs and wonders, and with all wicked deception for those who are perishing, because they refused to love the truth and so be saved. Therefore *God sends them a strong delusion*, so that they may believe what is false, in order that all may be condemned who did not believe the truth but had pleasure in unrighteousness. (2 Thessalonians 2:9–12 ESV, emphasis added)

A Buddhist in Africa who was converted to Christianity was asked why he changed religions. He replied, "It's like this; if you were walking along and came to a fork in the road and two men were there and one was dead and the other alive, which man's directions would you follow?"

"Let's be clear . . . that the claims of Christianity are in essence the claims of Christ," writes John Stott. "I have no particular wish to defend 'Christianity' as a system or 'the church' as an institution. The history of the church has been a bittersweet story, combining deeds of heroism with deeds of shame. But we are not ashamed of Jesus Christ, who is the center and core of Christianity. . . . Jesus believed he was unique, and it is this self-consciousness of Jesus that we need to investigate further."[19]

Apologist Ravi Zacharias has investigated Him and concludes, "This Jesus, whom I encountered in a moment of experience, I have tested through years of study and of seeking understanding. His description of the nature of reality and of everything within my own heart conforms to every test for truth to which I have submitted the teaching."[20]

If the Christ of the New Testament had not existed, no one would have invented Him; indeed, no one *could* have invented Him. When the chief priests and Pharisees sent officers to arrest Christ, they returned empty-handed. When pressed for an explanation, they replied, "No one ever spoke like this man!" (John 7:46 ESV). Either we are judged by this man, or we judge Him.

The choice we make determines our destiny.

FIVE: A SCIENTIFIC REASON

SCIENCE SUPPORTS BIBLICAL CREATION

In the beginning God created the heavens and the earth."
In these ten words we have the foundation for all scientific discovery. "In the beginning" introduces the concept of *time;* this refers to a specific point in a continuum when creation took place. "God" is the basis for *personality;* "created" introduces us to the concept of *energy,* those forces in the universe that play such a large part in explaining life and the secrets of the planets. Finally, "the heavens" refers to the vast regions of *space,* and "earth" affirms the existence of *matter.*

Looked at in different light, this single verse refutes all alternative philosophies regarding the origin and meaning of the universe. In his book *The Genesis Record,* Henry M. Morris points out that this opening statement of Genesis refutes (1) *atheism* because the universe was created by God. It refutes (2) *pantheism,* for God is transcendent to that which He created. It refutes (3) *polytheism,* for one God created all things. It refutes (4) *materialism,* for matter had a beginning. It refutes (5) *dualism,* for God was alone when He created. It refutes (6) *humanism,* for God, not man, is the ultimate reality. It refutes (7) *evolution* because God created all things.[1]

God existed before this "beginning." In other words, there never was time when only *nothing* existed. The biblical concept of creation involved a plan, a designer who began the process with an end in view. This designer *always was.*

Later in this chapter we shall give reasons to believe that the designer is best identified as the God of the Bible.

Some atheists, like Richard Dawkins and Daniel Dennett, see a problem here: Who designed the designer? Or who caused God?

Yet only "things that *begin* to exist must have causes," as William Lane Craig explains (emphasis added):[2]

"*In fact, Dennett himself recognizes that* a being 'outside of time . . . is nothing with an initiation or origin in need of explanation. What does need its origin explained is the concrete Universe itself.'[3] Dennett rightly sees that a being which exists eternally, since it never comes into being, has no need of a cause, as do things which have an origin."

Still, former physics and astronomy professor Victor Stenger maintains, "We see little resemblance in Genesis to the picture drawn by contemporary science. All these facts can lead to only one conclusion: the biblical version of creation is dead wrong." Presumably, by "contemporary science," he means Darwinian evolution. He appears to have ignored another possible conclusion, that Darwinism is dead wrong.[4]

If you do not believe that God created all that is, you must either believe that (1) there once was nothing, but from this nothing something came about or (2) there is no explanation for the existence of the universe, and whatever life we see around us has arisen from impersonal, random forces.

The first of these alternatives is not seriously held by anyone. It is unthinkable that from absolutely nothing, something should arise. But the second, that the universe as we know it arose by chance from some pre-existent matter, has gained plausibility.

This atheistic view would affirm that matter is eternal and from it everything has arisen. If we ask why there was matter in the first place, the answer is that there is no rational "cause" for its existence. Matter just always existed, and the universe as we see it today created itself without the help of an intelligent, personal deity. There was a time, it is said, when all matter and energy were concentrated in a tiny region of space much smaller than the nucleus of an atom! Then there was a "big bang," and a chain reaction formed the universe!

The scientific basis for the "big bang" theory dates back to 1929 when the astronomer Edwin Powell Hubble proved that the universe is constantly expanding. The galaxies are moving farther away from us and from each other. Suppose you were to take a marker and draw some galaxies on a balloon; as you blow it up, the "galaxies" move farther away from their starting point and farther from each other.

This discovery of an expanding universe led scientists to believe that the universe began at a single point in space and time. The late high priest of scientism, Carl Sagan, presented the big bang theory as a fact and taught that the entire universe resulted from a cosmic explosion 15 billion years ago;

all matter and energy were present at this massive "blowup." From this random, impersonal beginning, the complex forms of life that now exist developed.

This theory, often presented as fact, is now taught in our university textbooks. For example, *The Young Oxford Book of Astronomy* agrees with Sagan, that in the very beginning of the universe, all matter and radiation were concentrated into a tiny region of space much smaller than the nucleus of a single atom. Then it all began. "By the time the universe was about a millionth of a second old, much of the energy had been converted into protons (the nuclei of hydrogen atoms). In the next millisecond electrons formed, and these collided with the protons to make neutrons. Neutrons survive only a thousand seconds as independent particles, so the next few minutes were crucial!"[5]

What happened then? "Within the first quarter of an hour the protons reacted with the neutrons, which were fast decaying, to make the nuclei of helium atoms. In a race against time, as the universe continued to cool and expand, the universe managed to convert about a quarter of its matter to form hydrogen into helium. The remaining hydrogen was used to make the stars."[6]

This creation, the authors contend, was not out of nothing, but to use their words, "from next to nothing." Obviously, those first few seconds were crucial, since the random forces could have created something much less structured than our intricate universe. Given all of the possibilities, it is indeed a stroke of luck that intelligence and design should arise from impersonal forces. Noted physicist Stephen Hawking wrote, "If the rate of expansion one second after the big bang had been smaller by even one part in a hundred thousand million, the universe would have recollapsed before it ever reached its present state."[7]

Breathtaking!

Physicist Joel Primack, a professor at the University of California at Santa Cruz, agrees that the basic forces of nature split off from one unified force a few moments after the big bang, more than 15 billion years ago. That splitting could have happened in many different ways, only a few of which would have resulted in the inhabitable planets such as the earth.

"Humans seem to hit the jackpot in a 'Cosmic Las Vegas,'" he said, "leaving room for the possibility that some divine providence was responsible for our luck."[8]

A cosmic jackpot indeed! Edward P. Tyron, professor of physics at the City University of New York, even suggested that the original matter created itself. He said, "In 1973 I proposed that our universe had been created spontaneously from nothing (ex nihilo) as a result of established principles of physics. This proposal variously struck people as preposterous, enchanting or both."[9] Enchanting, perhaps; preposterous most certainly!

Many scientists have fought the notion of the big bang, fearing that it might play into the hands of creationists. As Sir Fred Hoyle, who dislikes the idea of creation, put it, "The big bang theory requires a recent origin of the Universe that openly invites the concept of creation."[10] Or, to quote Barry Parker, "If we accept the big bang theory, and most cosmologists now do, then a 'creation' of some sort is forced upon us."[11] George Smoot, a committed atheist, admitted, "There is no doubt that a parallel exists between the big bang as an event and the Christian notion of creation from nothing."[12]

Yes, there is a parallel. Christians are not in the unhappy position of believing what is contrary to all known laws of science, namely that matter can create itself, or that through random blind chance and natural selection it can organize itself into complex arrangements needed for life. In fact, the biblical explanation for the existence of the universe is by far more rational, more believable, and more scientific.

In addition, "The success of the West, including the rise of science, rested entirely on religious foundations, and the people who brought it about were devout Christians," sociologist Rodney Stark said.[13]

Oxford professor Alister McGrath was an atheist when he trained as a molecular biophysicist and planned a life in scientific research. Then he discovered Christianity and became a theologian. In his book *The Dawkins Delusion*, he scathingly rebuts the dogmatic atheism of fellow Oxford academic Richard Dawkins. He says Dawkins "made the transition from a scientist with a passionate concern for truth to a crude anti-religious propagandist who shows a disregard for evidence"—for which Dawkins has become something of an embarrassment even among some fellow atheists.[14]

"Most unbelieving scientists of my acquaintance are atheists on grounds other than their science; they bring those assumptions *to* their science rather than basing them *on* their science," McGrath writes.[15]

Dogmatic atheist scientists like Dawkins and Stenger claim science has proved that God does not exist, but that's hardly the consensus of the scientific community.

The more widely held view among scientists, says McGrath, is that science has its limits. The big questions of life, like how or why the universe began, the meaning of life, the existence of God, cannot be answered by science with any degree of certainty.

"Nature is open to many legitimate interpretations," he writes. "It can be interpreted in atheist, deist, theist, and many other ways—but it does not demand to be interpreted in any of these.... This, I may add, is the view of most scientists I speak to, including those who self-define as atheists."[16]

"The fundamental issue confronting the sciences is how to make sense of a highly complex, multifaceted, multilayered reality.... It pulls the rug out from under those who want to talk simplistically about scientific 'proof' or 'disproof' of such things.... There can be no question of scientific 'proof' of ultimate questions. Either we cannot answer them or we must answer them on grounds other than the sciences."[17]

Of course the Bible does speak to these ultimate questions, represents itself as God's own Word on them, and even goes so far as to state that those who observe this complex, multifaceted, multilayered reality that is life and the universe are "without excuse" for not seeing God, and His eternal power and divine nature, in all of it (Romans 1:19–22).

Atheist Sam Harris writes, "How the process of evolution got started is still a mystery, but that does not in the least suggest that a deity is likely to be lurking at the bottom of it. Any honest reading of the biblical account of creation suggests that God created all animals and plants as we now see them. There is no question that the Bible is wrong about this."[18]

"All complex life on earth has developed from simpler life-forms over billions of years. This is a fact that no longer admits of intelligent dispute." Thus he dismisses the scientists who dispute him as lacking in intelligence, their views not worth engaging.[19]

"We know that the universe is far older than the Bible suggests. We know that all complex organisms on earth, including ourselves, evolved from earlier organisms over the course of billions of years. The evidence for this is utterly overwhelming."[20] He simply repeats questionable, much-debated assertions with absolute certitude ("no question"), yet gives little, if any, evidence for them.

Such forceful assertion combined with weak evidence characterizes Dawkins's *God Delusion* as well, as McGrath describes: "Dawkins substitutes turbocharged rhetoric and highly selective manipulation of facts for evidence-based thinking" in his book. "Curiously, there is little scientific analysis in *The God Delusion*. . . . There's a lot of pseudoscientific speculation."[21]

"In short it is not as though Christians have faith, while secularists base their convictions purely on facts and reason. Secularism itself is based on ultimate beliefs, just as much as Christianity is. Some part of creation—usually matter or nature—functions in the role of the divine. So the question is not which view is religious and which is purely rational; the question is which is true and which is false," says Nancy Pearcey.[22]

Christian theology maintains that there are two "books": the book of God's written revelation and the book of nature. These "books" cannot contradict one another. Science, properly studied, is a study of the works of God. The purpose of this chapter is to show the harmony between science and the Bible, the harmony between the *words* of God and the *works* of God.

In creation God went public. "The heavens are telling of the glory of God; and their expanse is declaring the work of His hands" (Psalm 19:1). Science is just one more reason to believe that the Bible is the Word of God. As we shall see, the biblical account of the creation of the earth, moon, sun, and stars best explains the delicate relationship that exists between them. It is not just *difficult* to believe that the universe created itself, it is *impossible* to believe it. Nor can we believe that some form of eternal matter can explain what we know about the universe and ourselves. As we shall show, the greater our respect for science, the greater our respect for the Scriptures.

Later we shall also answer the question: If the universe points to a Creator, why should we ascribe this feat to the God of the Bible rather than some other deity?

HOW GOD PREPARED THE EARTH FOR MAN

The Bible teaches that God chose to create a stage upon which a drama would be enacted, and you and I are a part of the scene. The scientific data has helped all of us appreciate the uniqueness of our habitat. Here we see intelligence, purpose, and wisdom.

The Earth

"In the beginning God created the heavens and the earth. The earth was formless and void, and darkness was over the surface of the deep, and the Spirit of God was moving over the surface of the waters" (Genesis 1:1–2). The earth is a speck in a vast universe, but it is uniquely designed for life in general, and human life in particular. It is a huge ball covered with water, rock, and soil, surrounded by air.

When we are driving a car, we know that we are moving because objects outside are whistling past us. But when we are standing on the earth, we have no sensation of movement, because everything that surrounds us comes with us on our speedy journey. And what a journey it is!

The earth is like a baseball hurtling along in an elliptical movement around the sun, but it is also spinning at the same time. In fact it is orbiting the sun at the enormous speed of

19 miles every second, or about 66,000 miles every hour. It makes this journey of 595 million miles every year; every 365 days, 6 hours, 9.54 seconds, to be precise. (We need an extra day every four years of leap year to account for the extra quarter day in the earth's orbit. Without this correction the earth would be at a different point against the background of stars every January 1 and all successive dates.) These revolutions around the sun are punctual, never missing a second.

The axis of the earth (that imaginary line that connects the north and south poles) does not stick straight up in relation to the sun but actually tilts about 23 ½ degrees; it is this tilt that causes the seasons. For example, the northern half of the earth tilts toward the sun in summer and away from the sun in winter, resulting in the four seasons.

While speeding through space at 66,000 miles an hour, the earth is also spinning at some 1,000 miles an hour at the equator, revolving on its axis every 24 hours. This spinning motion makes it appear to us that the sun moves from east to west, and it causes day and night on the earth.

If we ask what causes the earth, moon, and sun to be in such a predictable relationship, scientists say it is gravity; if it were not for this force, the heavenly bodies would all fly off into space. If we ask a scientist what gravity actually is, we are told that it is the result of the presence of matter warping the space-time continuum. The earth's magnetic field results from electricity flowing within the earth's inner core. But we still don't totally understand gravity or the magnetic field. What amazes us is that gravity acts predictably in the heavens as well as on earth. Indeed, as far as we know, it is consistent throughout the whole universe.

The earth is special because it has the ingredients needed for life. For example, it has the compound water along with carbon and seventeen other chemical elements needed to build simple bacteria. And for advanced life forms, such as humans, we must add another nine elements! These ingredients must be brought together in a liquid water environment.[23]

Christians have always insisted that if life were found on other planets, this discovery would not conflict with the Bible. After all, if God wanted to create life, or even a civilization somewhere else, that certainly is His prerogative. However, most of us have the strong suspicion that the earth just might be the only place God chose to create life. This is the place He chose for the drama.

Some scientists are so anxious to believe that there is life on other planets that they are willing to accept almost any evidence, no matter how tenuous. A piece of rock found in Antarctica was heralded as proof that life could have evolved elsewhere. Why this rush to judgment? Remember: Materialists, committed to the evolutionary theory, are passionately interested in finding evidence that blind chance worked wonders elsewhere too. Life somewhere else would prove, they say, that matter can get organized and develop well beyond its known capacities on another planet. Since that time, articles have appeared in scientific journals debunking the idea that the rock found in Antarctica is evidence of the possibility of life on other planets.

The possibility that there is life on other planets is highly improbable. A star like the sun is needed to maintain life, but such stars are not common; only about 4 percent of the stars in the Milky Way fit a similar description and only 0.2 percent of the stars (called "G2") actually have such a capacity. Most stars would be disqualified to serve as a sun because they have a low abundance of heavy elements, lack the necessary radiation, and demonstrate inconsistency in brightness and output.[24]

Add to that the conditions actually needed for life on a given planet itself, and the possibility of life is, for all practical purposes, reduced to zero.

Even the size of the earth is crucial. Scientists tell us that if the earth were just 10 percent bigger or 10 percent smaller, life as we know it could not survive.

Not just any planet will do; not just any star will do. Not just any moon will do; not just any arrangement will do.

The Moon

"Then God said, 'Let there be lights in the expanse of the heavens to separate the day from the night, and let them be for signs and for seasons and for days and years; and let them be for lights in the expanse of the heavens to give light on the earth'; and it was so. God made the two great lights, the greater light to govern the day, and the lesser light to govern the night; He made the stars also" (Genesis 1:14–16).

The moon travels around the earth once about every 29.5 days and is the earth's only natural satellite and constant companion. It follows the earth as it makes its yearly journey around the sun. It has a diameter that is only about a fourth of that of the earth. If the moon sat next to the earth, it would look like a tennis ball next to a basketball.

Two forces balance the distance of the moon and the earth. Gravity tries to pull the earth and the moon toward each other; and at the same time, the centrifugal force of their rotation tries to pull the moon farther from the earth and throw it into space.

An illustration might help. We all probably have tied a string to a ball, then swung the ball in a circle. The centrifugal force makes the ball pull outward on the string. But the string, like gravity, keeps the ball from flying away.[25] Because gravity and centrifugal force are never balanced, the moon's distance and speed change. And yet it rotates around the earth in exactly 29.5 days and has been doing so since scientists were able to record its movements.

The moon's gravity affects the earth and the water that is closest to the moon, forming tides; when the moon is on the opposite side of the earth it pulls the solid body of the earth away from the water. As a result, two bulges called "high tides" are formed in the oceans and seas. These tides are necessary, for without the moon the tilt of the earth on its axis would be much less stable. It is the moon's gravity that maintains the earth's tilt near 23 ½ degrees. Without this tilt the temperature variations on the earth's surfaces would have been much greater.

Have you thanked God for Jupiter recently? Jupiter keeps comets from continually hitting the earth. Its powerful gravity alters the trajectories of these icy bodies so that most of them are flung out of the inner solar system. Without Jupiter the impact rate of comets on the earth would be about a thousand times greater.

The Sun

The sun is our closest star. The earth's volume would fit into the sun about 1 million times. Yet because the sun is four hundred times farther away than the moon, this "accident of nature," as one scientist puts it, makes the sun and moon appear about the same size in the sky.

The light of the sun comes from a layer in its atmosphere about three hundred miles thick. This energy was originally deep inside the sun but has now come to the surface. The temperature on the sun's surface is about ten thousand degrees

Fahrenheit. If the sun were closer to the earth we would die of heat; if it were farther away we would freeze. Or if it did not emit just the right amount of energy, life cycles would be thrown off-kilter. We live by the delicate balance of distances between the planets in our solar system, and particularly our distance from the sun.

The sun does not rotate like a solid body, such as the earth. Since it is a ball of gas, different parts rotate at different rates. The equator takes some twenty-five days for one rotation; closer to the poles, the rotation takes about thirty-five days. This difference in rotations helps wind up the sun's magnetic field, which increases its solar activity.

What were to happen if the sun were to distribute its light unevenly? That happens when there are what are known as "solar explosions," when the sun blasts out more energy. Back in 1987, such an explosion damaged electrical power stations in North America. If these high-energy particles were to continue for any length of time, the human body would be damaged.[26]

We can be grateful that the variations in the sun's light are minor in comparison to that of thousands of variable stars. Over a long period (perhaps a year or more) these stars become too dim to be seen, then slowly reappear. If the sun were that irregular, life on earth would come to an abrupt end. Imagine waking up each morning and discovering that the sun was growing dimmer each day. Even if it were to reappear more brightly within a few months, it would be too late.

As *The Young Oxford Book of Astronomy* says, "The Sun, the Moon and the Earth carry out a complex 'dance' in space. Sometimes all three end up almost in a straight line. This is when the fun of hide-and-seek starts, and you may be able to see an eclipse."[27] Yet, this "dance" is never random. The relationship between the earth, sun, moon, and stars is so predictable that an eclipse can be pinpointed hundreds of years in advance.

As for the sun itself, it has a family of eight planets, along with many smaller bodies, such as dwarf planets, asteroids, and comets. Gravity holds this family together as each planet moves in an elliptical orbit around the sun. Professor Robert Jastrow has stated that the smallest change in any of the relative strengths of the forces of nature, a change in the properties of the elementary particles, would have led to a universe in which there would be no life and no humans.[28] *The perfect, purposeful laws point to a perfect, purposeful superintelligence.*

"You alone are the Lord. You have made the heavens, the heaven of heavens with all their host, the earth and all that is on it, the seas and all that is in them. You give life to all of them and the heavenly host bows down before You" (Nehemiah 9:6).

The Stars

The stars you see at midnight in January are completely different from those you can see at midnight in July. Each night there are small but noticeable changes; the starry sky looks like distant scenery enveloping the earth and the whole solar system. If we could travel into space we would see stars in every direction against the black sky. Astronauts can see the stars below them as well as above, for the stars exist in all directions.

Anyone who looks into the sky soon begins to link the brighter stars into simple patterns, triangles, crosses, or arches. These patterns have triggered many imaginations, and thus the ancients who mapped out the heavens divided the heavenly bodies into constellations.

The size of the stars and their distances from us strain the limits of our imagination. We've learned that our sun is a star, but it is nearby, only 93 million miles from us. The next nearest star is 250,000 times farther away! If we could take a ride on a spaceship traveling at the speed of light it would take us eight minutes to get to the sun and four years to get to the next nearest star! All that while traveling 186,000 miles every second!

Or think of it this way. Take a sheet of paper and draw a sun, say the size of a golf ball, on the top of the paper. Then put a dot representing the earth on the bottom of your sheet. If you were to represent the closest star in the stellar universe, your next circle would have to be forty miles away!

If we kept traveling in our spaceship at the speed of light, we could do so for a hundred years, then a thousand, then a hundred thousand, then a million, then millions upon millions of years. After about 20 billion years, we would be at the outskirts of the universe. Beyond that, there are many uncertainties; we don't know how far the universe might continue. But we must remember that light from the remotest parts of the universe set out on its journey a long time ago and is just arriving now. The light of other stars is still on its way; it has not yet arrived.

God told Abraham that if he could number the stars, he would also be able to count the number of his seed. God's point was not that Abraham would have as many descendants as there are stars, but rather that neither can be counted.

We can't grasp the number of the stars, but we can try. Our own Milky Way, the galaxy to which our own sun belongs, has about 100 billion stars. Its diameter is about 100,000 light-years, small in comparison to other galaxies. This galaxy has satellite galaxies, and there are other clusters of galaxies, with different shapes and sizes. It is estimated that there are about 10 million galaxies, each with hundreds of millions of stars. Indeed, there are more stars, we are told, than there are grains of sand on the seashores of the earth. Yet, God knows each one by name (Psalm 147:4).

We are faced with a decision: Do we believe that the universe came to be "from next to nothing" and that we hit a "cosmic jackpot," or that God spoke and the universe was created with order, design, and predictability? Indeed, Princeton physicist Freeman Dyson says that the more he examines the universe and the details of its architecture, the more evidence he finds that "the universe in some sense must have known that we were coming."[29]

It is difficult to believe that an impersonal universe itself knew we were coming, but *Someone certainly did!*

IDENTIFYING THE CREATOR

What kind of a God would be qualified to be the cause of all that we know about the universe? First, He would have to be a God of awesome *power.* The universe is an effect that demands a very great cause. Since the cause must be greater than the effect, God must be supremely powerful.

Second, this God must be *personal,* possessing intelligence and will. The pantheistic gods of the East are impersonal, indifferent to good and evil, uninvolved in planning and judging; such gods are "the force" but not the personal creator. Thus, if we adopt the view of the East, we have no explanation for personality.

In contrast, the biblical God created man in His own image; that is, possessing a godlikeness. Yet, man is not God, nor an extension of Him. We are independent of God, yet have intellect, will, and emotion. In contrast, the evolutionary view says that even thought itself is the interaction of blind forces of physics and chemistry. Incredibly, evolutionists believe that matter can think! It is much more scientific, and makes more sense, to believe that it takes an intelligent personality to create intelligent personalities.

Third, the God who created the universe must *exist outside of time;* for us humans, time is measured by the motion of heavenly bodies. The Bible teaches that before there was any matter, before there was any material to generate the big bang, the Creator was there. God declares that He is without beginning and end: "I AM" (Exodus 3:14). Indeed, David wrote that before God brought the worlds into being, "From everlasting to everlasting, You are God" (Psalm 90:2).

This God is not, however, simply the Creator who put certain laws of gravity into motion and then left His creation. The universe, including the earth and all that is within it, depends continually upon the mercy of Christ who "upholds all things by the word of His power" (Hebrews 1:3). Scientists tell us that the universe would collapse into a small ball of matter were it not for the continual forces of gravity that keep the electrons in motion. Moment by moment God sustains the universe.

Finally, the God who *created* would also have the right to *bring His creation to an abrupt halt* whenever He chooses. If He is not only powerful, but also moral, He can if He desires judge those creatures created in His image. Here, again, the Christian God best fits this description.

"But the heavens and the earth, which are now, by the same word are kept in store, reserved unto fire against the day of judgment and perdition of ungodly men" (2 Peter 3:7 KJV). The biblical teaching is that He brought heaven and earth into existence, and the same Word that created will be the same Word that will judge. God speaks, doing what He wills. Yes, He "knew we were coming"!

THE CONFESSIONS OF SCIENTISTS

Minds more brilliant than ours have pondered the immensity of the universe and its intricate designs. Many have concluded that the universe does not have within itself the cause of its own existence. Listen to the words of those who have grasped the wonder of the created order.

- *Albert Einstein.* "The scientist is possessed by the sense of universal causation. . . . His religious feeling takes the form of rapturous amazement at the harmony of natural law, which reveals an intelligence of such superiority that, compared with it, all the systematic thinking and acting of human beings is an utterly insignificant reflection."
- *Sir Fred Hoyle, astrophysicist.* "A common sense interpretation of the facts suggests that a super-intellect has monkeyed with physics, as well as with chemistry and biology, and that there are no blind forces worth speaking about in nature. The numbers one calculates from the facts seem to me so overwhelming as to put this conclusion almost beyond question."
- *Robert Jastrow, astronomer.* "For the scientist who has lived by his faith in the power of reason, the story ends like a bad dream. He has scaled the mountains of ignorance; he is about to conquer the highest peak; as he pulls himself over the final rock, *he is greeted by a band of theologians who have been sitting there for centuries*" (emphasis added).[30]

Finally, we have a quote from the late Carl Sagan, a dedicated atheist. He admits, "It is easy to see that only a very restricted range of laws of nature are consistent with galaxies and stars, planets, life and intelligence."[31] Yes, and the logical conclusion is that these highly ordered laws were created by a highly ordered superintelligence.

Such an admission is more than some scientists who cling to evolutionary beliefs can make though, as Phillip Johnson, a Christian professor, describes: "When I tell my fellow Berkeley professors that I don't believe the theory of evolution, I need to know why they find it so difficult to take me seriously or to believe that my objection to the theory is based on scientific evidence rather than on the book of Genesis. The reason is that evolution with its accompanying philosophy is identified with their worldview at such a deep level that they cannot imagine how the theory could possibly be contrary to the evidence."[32]

The Bible harmonizes with the theory of relativity. "With the Lord one day is like a thousand years, and a thousand years like one day" (2 Peter 3:8). It also agrees with the first law of thermodynamics that the amount of matter in the universe is constant; none is being created or destroyed. "By the seventh day God completed His work which He had done, and He rested on the seventh day from all His work which He had done" (Genesis 2:2). Finally, the Bible substantiates the second law of thermodynamics, that the universe is becoming less ordered. It is "wearing out." The author of Hebrews says that in the beginning the Lord created the heavens and the earth, but "they all will become old like a garment, and like a mantle you will roll them up" (Hebrews 1:11–12).[33]

Only the Bible has its cosmology right. Only an eternal, omnipotent God could give this universe its beginning and sustain it; only a personal God could account for personal beings. "For by Him all things were created, both in the heavens and on earth, visible and invisible, whether thrones or dominions or rulers or authorities—all things have been created through Him and for Him. He is before all things, and in Him all things hold together" (Colossians 1:16–17).

GOD AT HIS BEST

Perhaps you have heard the late California Pastor E. V. Hill's sermon, "When Was God at His Best?" Theologians would want to remind us that God is *always* at His best; He does all things with excellence and purpose. But Hill's point, I think, lay in a different direction: when do *we* see God at His best? Not in the creation of the worlds, awesome though that is.

For us, God was at His best when He reconciled us to Himself and performed a creative miracle within us. "Therefore if anyone is in Christ, he is a new creature; the old things passed away; behold, new things have come" (2 Corinthians 5:17). Both the physical creation and the spiritual creation are miracles from the same Lord. In the Scriptures, creation and redemption are combined; both are the work of God.

First, both creations were *ex nihilo*, that is, without the help of preexisting material. "For God, who said, 'Let light shine out of darkness,' has shone in our hearts to give the light of the knowledge of the glory of God in the face of Jesus Christ" (2 Corinthians 4:6 esv). The new nature of believers comes about through the creative energy of God. When we were re-created at conversion, something is now with us that was not there before. God spoke, and a new nature was formed within those of us who have believed in His Son.

Second, both creations took place without human aid. Obviously, no one was there to help God when the worlds were created; and although we are present when God creates a new nature within us, it was His act alone. We could no more cooperate with Him than a dead man can cooperate in effecting his own resurrection. Yes, of course we must believe in Christ to be saved, but even the faith we have is God's gift. And the miracle of regeneration (that is, receiving the life of God) is wholly His work in our hearts.

This explains why Christians insist that the death of Christ on the cross was even a greater display of God's power than the creation of the universe. Attributes of God, previously hidden from us, burst forth with clarity. Nature tells us of God's power and intelligence but nothing of grace, mercy, and love. With the death of Christ, God proved that He could remain just and yet be the "justifier" of those who believe on Jesus. Here power, grace, and glory met to show His wondrous condescension.

The so-called conflict between science (the physical creation) and religion (the spiritual re-creation) simply does not exist. It is impossible for the Bible to contradict science since God is the author of both. If we are pressed to explain generations of conflict, the answer is (1) that those who believe the Bible have often crafted interpretations that were not based on a careful study of the text. Needless to say, the earth was not created in 4004 BC as the study notes in one Bible affirm. Many of us hold to a "young earth," but since the Bible does not tell us when God created the heavens and the earth, we must respect those who believe that the earth is much older than some creationists have believed.

Then (2) some Christian scholars have gone to the other extreme, attempting to make concessions to the evolutionary theory that are both unnecessary, and some would say, unscientific. Hybrid theories abound, such as the "Day-Age theory" or "Progressive Creationism," which can be generally classified as "Theistic Evolution." Obviously, there is room for debate in all these matters, but evolution as it is generally taught stands in direct opposition to Christianity. Certainly there may be a form of evolution within species, but Darwinism is so antiscientific that there is no need to try to harmonize it with the Bible.

Finally, (3) the conflict has escalated because so many scientists are committed to a naturalistic explanation of origins. If one takes the position that God did not—or indeed *could not*—have a role in creation, then the outcome of all scientific study is predictable. As evolutionist D. M. S. Watson candidly admitted, evolution is "a theory universally accepted not because it can be proven by logically coherent evidence to be true, but because the only alternative, special creation, is clearly incredible."[34]

David saw the heavens as leading him toward God and not away from Him. And although he lived centuries before the rise of modern science, we should take a page from his book in Psalm 8:3–4, 9.

> When I consider Your heavens, the work of Your fingers,
> The moon and the stars, which You have ordained;
> What is man that You take thought of him,
> And the son of man, that You care for him? . . .
> O Lord, our Lord,
> How majestic is Your name in all the earth!

FOR FURTHER CONSIDERATION

The Demise of Evolution

Today evolution is severely discredited by many scientists and philosophers, though a number of avowedly atheistic scientists zealously defend it. What was once considered a sacred dogma is now being seen without the veneer and verbal hype used to prop up the theory. Evolution not only has changed from the time of Darwin, but it is in disarray.

Many scientists are now admitting that evolution is contrary to known laws of science and therefore is not based on science but on naturalism, the belief exposed by Carl Sagan, who said, "The Cosmos is all there ever was or ever will be." Evolution, if it is anything, is antiscientific.

Have you ever felt frustrated because it is clear to you that evolution is impossible, and you wonder why people hold to the theory with religious fervor? You marvel that there are actually some scientists who believe that nothing times nobody equals everything. You marvel that they can believe that impersonal matter could become highly organized on its own and "create" intelligence and purposefully sustain life. Yet, even in the face of overwhelming evidence to the contrary, evolutionists remain convinced.

I used to think that if scientists were presented with the impossibilities of the evolutionary theory, they would concede, admitting that it is not only improbable, but also impossible. Some, of course, have changed their minds; others, however, will not abandon the theory no matter how antiscientific it can be shown to be.

Phillip Johnson has helped all of us understand why evolution is still believed, regardless of evidence to the contrary. In his helpful book *Darwin on Trial*[35] he shows that evolutionists are first of all committed to a materialistic view of the universe and only secondarily to the scientific enterprise. In other words, they see it as their duty to get people to accept the right starting point, namely, to reject all supernatural explanations of origins and accept as fact the findings of "evolutionary science." Once that point is made, evolution is believed even if it can be shown to be contrary to the science it purports to exalt. No wonder Dr. Lewis Bounoure, Director of Scientific Research in France, is quoted as saying, "Evolution is a fairy tale for adults."[36]

To show how a commitment to materialism overrides a commitment to science in the mind of evolutionists, Philip Johnson quotes the evolutionist Lewontin, who explains why we should reject creationism out of hand. Lewontin writes:

> We take the side of science in spite of the patent absurdity of some of its constructs, in spite of its failure to fulfill many of its extravagant promises of health and life, in spite of the tolerance of the scientific community for unsubstantiated just-so stories, because we have a prior commitment, a commitment to materialism. It is not that the methods and institutions of science somehow compel us to accept a material explanation of the phenomenal world, but on the contrary, that we are forced by our a priori adherence to material causes to create an apparatus of investigation and a set of concepts that produce material explanations, no matter how counterintuitive, no matter how mystifying to the uninitiated. Moreover, that materialism is absolute, for we cannot allow a Divine Foot in the door. The eminent Kant scholar Lewis Beck used to say that anyone who could believe in God could believe in anything. To appeal to an omnipotent deity is to allow that at any moment the regularities of nature may be ruptured, that miracles may happen.[37]

So there you have it: *If science does not support evolution, then science be damned!* Only this narrow-minded commitment to materialism can explain why some evolutionists will not abandon their theory regardless of the evidence. No matter how absurd, no matter how preposterous, even if it is a fairy tale for adults, it still must be believed! The alternative of creationism is unacceptable. In short, evolution must be believed, even if it is wrong!

There are three gaps evolution has not been able to bridge: (1) the gap between nothing and matter, (2) the gap between matter and life, and (3) the gap between man and the lower creation. To bridge these gaps evolutionists must adopt unscientific theories.

The Gap between Nothing and Matter

First, evolutionists must disregard a basic scientific premise, namely, that *from nothing, nothing comes.* Most evolutionists believe that matter always existed; to believe that it arose from nothing is contrary to logic and observation. Yet if matter is eternal as claimed, we have no reason for believing that it could have organized itself into complex forms well beyond its properties. We must humbly admit that the universe has purposefulness and power that cannot be accounted for within itself.

The Gap between Matter and Life

Evolution must disregard the second law of thermodynamics, namely, that the amount of available energy is depleting and that nature, when left to itself, tends toward randomness and disorganization. An evolutionist must believe that nonliving atoms slowly organized themselves into complex, energy-rich forms. Such a feat has never been observed in nature and is contrary to what we know from the law of cause and effect.

Scientist A. E. Wilder-Smith gives this example. If you were to take a small aircraft, fly it six thousand feet over your home, and throw out 100,000 white cards, what is the statistical possibility that they will land in such a way as to spell your initials? Obviously, the chances are nil. But an evolutionist would insist that given enough time, anything could happen. So, let us give the cards more time to fall by flying higher and attaching parachutes to each of the cards to give them longer time to fall to the earth. Does that increase the probability that your name will appear on the open field?

Or consider putting various bits of metal into a barrel and shaking it for a million years. What are the chances of forming a wristwatch? And if the millions of years turned out to be billions, would your chance be greater?

Remember a single cell has much more complexity than the initials of your name or even a wristwatch. Since the unraveling of the DNA code, we have a better appreciation for what would be needed to create a human being. Each person has approximately 30 trillion cells in his body. Each cell contains forty-six chromosomes (twenty-three from each parent). The activity within a single cell is equivalent to that of a large city, such as Chicago or Tokyo. Each cell has genetic information that programs it to become a part of one of the many different parts of the body. Walter T. Brown writes, "The genetic information contained in each cell of the human body is roughly equivalent to a library of 4,000 volumes."[38] If we multiply that by 30 trillion, we can begin to appreciate the complexity of every human being.

To assume that all of this was put together by chance is beyond belief. The late H. Quastler calculated the odds as 1 in 10 with 301 zeros. Mathematically that is equivalent to believing that there was an explosion in a print factory and the result was a Webster's dictionary! It does not matter how much time we give nature; the huge numerical odds simply are irrelevant: we must simply admit that no matter how much time and how much luck, evolution could not have happened.

In *Darwin's Black Box* Michael Behe, a biochemist, has shown conclusively that Darwinian evolution is impossible. Darwin advanced the notion that biological systems could have been advanced by numerous, successive, slight modifications. Behe, using a mousetrap, showed why that is impossible: you need all the parts of a mousetrap to catch a mouse. You can't catch a few mice with a platform, then later add a spring, catch a few more, and then add the hammer and improve the function. The mousetrap must have all of these elements before it can function. In the same way, human cells are irreducibly complex, and their life and function could not have slowly evolved. In other words, Darwinism, says Behe, flunks at the molecular level. Life, he says, can only be the product of intelligent design.

Consider the bombardier beetle, which defends itself by shooting out bad-smelling gases that ignite in the face of an enemy at 212 degrees Fahrenheit (as hot as boiling water). Sometimes the beetle sets off four or five of these "bombs" in quick succession. To accomplish this, two kinds of chemicals (hydrogen peroxide and hydroquinone) are used; if you went into a chemistry lab and mixed them together they would cause an explosion. Therefore, to carry these two chemicals together, the beetle has an inhibitor that prevents the chemicals from exploding even though they are stored in the same compartment.

In a separate compartment, an anti-inhibitor waits for

the right moment to neutralize the inhibitor. So at the exact moment the beetle wants to fire at an enemy, the anti-inhibitor is squirted through a tube to unite with the other two chemicals, which are squirted through their separate tube. This anti-inhibitor neutralizes the inhibitor so that the two chemicals are free to react violently together and explode.

Someone has suggested that we try to imagine how this beetle might have slowly evolved! An evolving beetle could hardly have experimented with the two chemicals or he would have been blown to bits! How could the inhibitor just evolve? There is no need for the inhibitor to evolve unless you first have the two chemicals; but if you have the chemicals without the inhibitor, it is too late. Someone had to know that the inhibitor was needed right from the start.

On the other hand, if the inhibitor had evolved, it would not have done the beetle any good. The solution would just sit and soak. So, does this mean that for thousands of years little beetles mixed the two chemicals for no good reason until an anti-inhibitor evolved? Someone had to know that the beetle needed both an inhibitor and an anti-inhibitor if it were to survive.

But even if the anti-inhibitor evolved, the poor little beetle would be blown up if it just added the anti-inhibitor. What it needs is two combustion tubes and a separate storage compartment for the anti-inhibitor, so that it can be used only when threatened. Added to this is the need for a complex communication system so that the anti-inhibitor is ejected at just the right time!

Behe wrote: "Both the bombardier beetle's defensive apparatus and the vertebrate eye contain so many molecular components (on the order of tens of thousands of different types of molecules) that listing them—and speculating on the mutations that might have produced them—is currently impossible."[39]

It was always said that evolution is improbable but "it happened." At last many scientists are admitting it is not only improbable, but also *impossible*. No wonder atheists are now speaking of "directed chance" or "biochemical predestination." C. S. Lewis called this kind of language a belief in a "tame god" who will not bother you. "All the thrills of religion and none of the cost," he said. Yes, evolution is a "god" for our times.

The Gap between Man and the Lower Creation

Every so often we are told there is a new "missing link" in the life chain between animal and man. Of course, if evolution had happened over millions of years, there would be tens of thousands of transitional fossils. Fact is, the haphazard fossil record simply does not support the theory.

But perhaps the greatest proof that naturalistic evolution cannot account for man is this: Evolutionists do not believe in the existence of the soul or mind because a spiritual substance cannot arise out of evolving matter. What we call the mind, they say, is just the product of physical and chemical changes in the brain; our thoughts are just a combination of calcium, phosphate, and other chemicals. Therefore, *evolutionists believe that matter can think.*

But if matter can think, we have no control or responsibility for what we think, since we do not control physical and chemical laws. Since we can't say that one combination of chemical reactions is better than another, all thoughts are morally neutral. Whatever is, is. Morality does not exist.

"In the unfolding narrative of the Bible, however, the divine image is clearly what distinguishes humans from animals, namely a cluster of unique human qualities," points out John Stott.[40] He names these qualities as capacities—for rational thought, for moral choice, for artistic creativity, for social relationships of love. These capacities "set us apart from animals and . . . together constitute the image of God in us."[41] What explanation seems more likely for these capacities? Darwinian science's, that they resulted from evolutionary processes, or the Bible's, that God created these in us?

Only a belief in a God who created man with a spiritual inner nature (that is, not subject to the laws of chemistry) can account for human responsibility. Regardless of how loudly evolutionists proclaim their atheism, they live and behave like men and women created in the image of God. "For since the creation of the world His invisible attributes, His eternal power and divine nature, have been clearly seen, being understood through what has been made, so that they are without excuse" (Romans 1:20).

The biblical account of creation is eminently scientific. Creation shouts "Behold your God!" to all who will listen.

GOD'S PEOPLE, BY HIS PROVIDENCE, RECOGNIZED THE CANON

Who decided what books would be in the Bible, and when did they do it?

Many people suppose that these decisions were made by a church council that met behind closed doors and debated the issues, accepting some books and rejecting others. Or else they surmise that these books "just happened" to be collected without any special criterion by which they would be judged worthy of Scripture. Neither perception is correct.

The purpose of this chapter is to answer commonly asked questions about the canon (the word originally meant a "rule" or "measuring rod" and refers to the official list of authoritative books accepted by Christians). Historians might not be able to answer all of our questions, but from what we do know, the formation of the canon shows the hand of divine providence. Even the agreement of the early church on the canon is one more reason to believe that the Bible is the Word of God.

Here are some questions we will attempt to answer in this chapter:

- Why should we believe that the church has the right list of inspired books?
- Why does the Roman Catholic Bible have additional books not found in Protestant Bibles?
- Why do Protestants believe that the Bible is the sole basis for faith and practice?

Any discussion of the canon quickly divides Protestants and Catholics. Not only do Catholics have more books in their Bible (see "For Further Consideration" at the end of this chapter), but they also view the Bible differently. That is why it is quite true to say that your opinion of the relationship between the canon and the church determines whether you are a Protestant or a Catholic.

Let me introduce Stephen and Janet Ray. When they converted from Protestantism to Roman Catholicism, their decision came down to this question: Does the church have authority over the canon, or does the canon have authority over the church? Catholicism teaches the primacy of the church over the canon of Scripture; it believes that the official church is just as infallible as the Bible. Indeed, Catholics believe that we could not have an infallible Bible if we did not have an infallible church.

The argument runs like this. The Bible alone cannot be our authority because the Bible does not tell us what books should be in the Bible. The church, that is, popes and councils, determined which books are in the Bible; therefore, *we must accept the authority of the church as infallible.*

To put it differently, if the church were fallible, it might have been in error regarding the books it selected. To quote Stephen Ray, "Protestants are dependent upon the tradition of the Catholic Church for their current New Testament."[1] When a Protestant friend of mine was explaining to a Catholic colleague that we are saved by faith in Christ alone, he responded, "You Protestants should remember that *it is the Catholic Church that gave you the Bible.*"

So, the argument is that if there is no final authority regarding what books are in the Bible, then any person or sect can accept or reject books as they please. To quote Ray again, "To be honest, those who recognize no binding ecclesiastical authority able to close the canon must respect *any* canon."[2] To repeat, Catholicism teaches that the church had to be infallible to give us an infallible canon.

Sometimes we as Protestants are prone to ask a Catholic, "Why do you pray to Mary since no such doctrine is found in the New Testament?" We are frustrated when they reply, "It does not matter whether it is in the Bible; the teaching of the church is just as binding as the Scriptures and even more so." The same goes for praying to saints, purgatory, and indulgences. Remember, the Catholic Church believes it has the right to adopt authoritative traditions, so for them the body of revealed truth extends well beyond the canon of Scripture.

Welcome to the debate about the canon!

HOW THE BIBLE CAME TO BE

The Bible is a remarkable collection of sixty-six books, united by a common theme, and like a tapestry it weaves together the story of God's redemption of the human race. That these books should be collected, agreed upon, and accepted as the Word of God is itself a miracle of God's providence. Sketching the big picture will help us put the details in perspective.

Stay with me as we review how the books of the Bible were collected and the relevance of this history for the debate about the canon. Then we will be in a better position to discuss some of these controversial questions.

The Old Testament Canon

When God authorized the writing of a manuscript, and the people of God recognized it as such, it was preserved. For example, Moses wrote "all the words of the Lord" (Exodus 24:4; see also Joshua 8:30–35), and these writings were carefully laid in the ark of the covenant (Deuteronomy 31:26); so were the writings of Joshua (Joshua 24:26) and Samuel, whose words were put "in the book and placed . . . before the Lord" (1 Samuel 10:25). The same can be said for Jeremiah (Daniel 9:2) and Daniel.

Obviously, the number of books increased and subsequent generations honored them as the Word of the Lord. For example, Ezra possessed a copy of the Law of Moses and the Prophets (Nehemiah 9:14, 26–30). This Law was read and revered as the Word of God.

Of course, not all Jewish religious literature was considered a part of the inspired list of books. For example the book of Jashar existed (Joshua 10:13) as well as the Book of the Wars of the Lord (Numbers 21:14) and others (1 Kings 11:41). These books have not survived the centuries, so we don't know their contents.

As the canon grew in size it often was described with the phrase "Moses and the Prophets," and later it was referred to as "the Law, Prophets, and Writings" (or "the Psalms"). Jesus Himself alluded to this threefold division when He spoke of "the Law of Moses and the Prophets and the Psalms" (Luke 24:44).

To be fair, we must report that the canonicity of five Old Testament books was questioned at one time or another, each for a different reason. For some, the Song of Solomon was too sensual; Ecclesiastes was too skeptical; and because Esther does not mention the name of God, some thought it too unspiritual. Some questioned Proverbs because some of the maxims seemed to contradict each other. And finally, some Jewish scholars thought Ezekiel was anti-Mosaic, and its visions were said to tend toward Gnosticism.

Despite these objections, most of the Jewish scholars did not question these books; they were regarded as canonical soon after they were written and, properly interpreted, are in complete harmony with the other books of the Old Testament. The centuries have proven the wisdom of keeping them within the biblical canon.

If you were to look at the table of contents of a Hebrew Old Testament, you would notice two differences from our English Old Testament. First, it has only twenty-two books, not thirty-nine. But it is most important to realize that the content is identical; it is just that the Hebrew Bible combines certain books. (For example, books such as 1 and 2 Samuel are combined into one; other smaller books are attached to larger ones.)

A second difference is that the order of the books is rearranged. Interestingly, the last book of the Hebrew Bible is not Malachi but Chronicles.

Now let me share an incidental proof that Christ's Bible was the same in content as the Hebrew Old Testament we have today. The first murder in the Old Testament was, of course, when Cain killed Abel; the last murder, according to the Hebrew order of books, was when the prophet Zechariah was stoned to death in the temple (2 Chronicles 24:20–21).

Only now are we prepared to understand the words of Jesus:

> Therefore, behold, I am sending you prophets and wise men and scribes; some of them you will kill and crucify, and some of them you will scourge in your synagogues, and persecute from city to city, so that upon you may fall the guilt of all the righteous blood shed on earth, from the blood of righteous Abel to the blood of Zechariah, the son of Berechiah, whom you murdered between the temple and the altar. (MATTHEW 23:34–35)

Given the order of the Hebrew Old Testament, Christ gives a sweeping panorama of its entire history. These two murders are "bookends" for the whole of the Hebrew canon. In New Testament terms we would say, "From Genesis to Revelation." This is further proof that Christ's Bible was that of the Jewish Hebrew canon (though arranged differently), from our own Old Testament.

Interestingly, eighteen out of the twenty-two books of the Hebrew canon are quoted as authoritative Scripture in the New Testament (all except Judges, Chronicles, Esther, and Song of Solomon). But by clear implication these books were also regarded as holy Scripture since Christ frequently referred to the whole Old Testament as a unit. And even when He said, "Do not think that I came to abolish the Law or the Prophets; I did not come to abolish but to fulfill"

(Matthew 5:17), He obviously had all of the Jewish Scriptures in mind.

The Jews agreed that the canon of the Old Testament closed in about 400 BC with the prophecy of Malachi. Indeed, the period between the Old Testament and the New is often referred to as "The Four Hundred Silent Years." God was not speaking directly to His people; no words of His were written down.

What can we know for sure? First, that our Old Testament is based on the Hebrew Old Testament that was accepted by the Jews. And second, that this is the same canon that Christ ratified by His frequent references to the Old Testament as the unbreakable Word of God. In giving His approval to these books whose content is identical to ours, we can be confident that the Old Testament canon is authoritative and closed.

Wherein do we see God's providence? Remember, these books were selected by the people of God without the benefit of a council that debated the merits of each book. The people of God themselves distinguished writings, sometimes discussing and disagreeing, but these decisions were never in the hands of a select committee.

Yes, there was a council that met in Jamnia in AD 95 and the canon of the Old Testament was on its agenda, but the council only ratified books that the Jews had already accepted five centuries earlier. The council neither rejected a single book nor did it add others to the list. The authentic books had already proved their worth; the wheat had already been separated from the chaff.

The New Testament Canon

The same authority we have noticed in the Old Testament is ascribed to the writers of the New Testament. Again, the authority of the Scriptures is not found in human brilliance or speculation but is rooted in the character of God. Paul could tell the congregation in Corinth that what he was writing to them was the Lord's command (1 Corinthians 14:37).

Jesus commissioned the disciples to pass on the truth He had taught them. "These things I have spoken to you while abiding with you. But the Helper, the Holy Spirit, whom the Father will send in My name, He will teach you all things, and bring to your remembrance all that I said to you" (John 14:25–26). Of course, we have to realize that the early church did not have a central worship center to house the books as the Jews did. Christianity spread beyond the bounds of Judaism and became an international religion; there was no special location that would serve as a central base of authority. Persecution scattered the church in all directions.

The books of the New Testament were written during the last half of the first century. Most of the books were written to local churches (for example, the majority of Paul's epistles were written to churches in Ephesus, Philippi, Colossae, etc.) and some were addressed to individuals. Other books, penned by various writers were written for a broader audience in eastern Asia (1 Peter), western Asia (Revelation), and even Europe (Romans).

With such geographical diversity of origin and destination it is understandable that not all the churches would immediately have copies of these various letters. With limitations of communication and travel, it is to be expected that time would pass before the number of books regarded as authoritative would be finally settled.

Obviously, there was a process of selection and verification done by the early believers. And as long as the apostles were alive everything could be checked out (Luke 1:2; Acts

1:21–22). For example, John could say, "The life was manifested, and we have seen and testify and proclaim to you the eternal life, which was with the Father and was manifested to us—what we have seen and heard we proclaim to you" (1 John 1:2–3). Peter assured us that he was an eyewitness of the transfiguration and that his description was based on firsthand evidence (2 Peter 1:16–18). Apostolic authority was a final court of appeal.

Just as books were added to the Old Testament canon, so the various books of the New Testament gained acceptance by the early church as they were written and circulated. Right from earliest times the church had a functional canon; that is, some books were accepted as authoritative even when others were not yet written.

Paul commanded the Thessalonians, "I adjure you by the Lord to have this letter read to all the brethren" (1 Thessalonians 5:27). And again to the Colossians he wrote, "When this letter is read among you, have it also read in the church of the Laodiceans" (Colossians 4:16). John promised a blessing for all who listened to the book of Revelation being read (Revelation 1:3). Clearly the apostolic letters were intended for the whole church. There was a kind of round-robin circulation of books that steadily grew.

That some books were accepted as Scripture soon after they were written can be confirmed by the words of Peter. He possessed a collection of Paul's letters and regarded them as Scripture. Listen to this amazing confirmation of Paul's authority. Peter wrote:

> Regard the patience of our Lord as salvation; just as also our beloved brother Paul, according to the wisdom given him, wrote to you, as also in all his letters, speaking in them of these things, in which are some things hard to

understand, which the untaught and unstable distort, as they do also the rest of the Scriptures, to their own destruction. (2 PETER 3:15–16)

Paul's letters were almost immediately regarded as authoritative.

Other books can be shown to have enjoyed the same acceptance. Jude quoted from Peter (Jude 17; cf. 2 Peter 3:2); Paul cited Luke's gospel as Scripture (1 Timothy 5:18; cf. Luke 10:7). Obviously, the believers of the early church recognized a growing body of literature as the inspired Word of God.

Yes, there were some disagreements. Hebrews was suspect in the minds of some because the authorship of the book is unknown, and some doubted that 2 Peter was written by Peter and thus ascribed it to an unknown author who borrowed his material from Jude. Revelation is missing from some early lists, probably because it was unknown in some places. Two books, thought by some to be canonical Scripture, were ultimately rejected. (See "For Further Consideration" at the end of this chapter.)

We can be grateful that once the present twenty-seven New Testament books were accepted, there have been no moves within the church to either delete some or add others. There are good reasons to believe that the early church correctly discerned the letters that came to them from God.

To summarize the development of the New Testament canon:

1. Letters from apostles were written and received in the churches; copies were made and circulated.

2. A growing group of books developed that were recognized as inspired Scripture. An important question for their acceptance was this: Was the book either written by an apostle or by someone who knew the apostles, and thus had the stamp of apostolic authority? For example, Luke was not an apostle, but he was a confidant and travel companion of Paul. We should also point out that the authorship of Hebrews was unknown, and yet the book was accepted. It bears such a powerful witness to Christ as the fulfillment of the Old Testament that the church became convinced of its authority.

3. By the end of the first century all twenty-seven books in our present canon were written and received by the churches.[3] Though some of the canonical lists were incomplete, this is not to be interpreted as the rejection of some books but often simply means that some books were unknown in certain areas.

4. To show both agreement and the widespread acceptance of the New Testament books, we should note that by a generation following the end of the apostolic age, every book of the New Testament had been cited as authoritative by some church father.[4]

5. Remaining doubts or debates over certain books continued into the fourth century. As far as historians know, the first time the list of our twenty-seven books appears is in an Easter letter written by Athanasius, an outstanding leader of the church in AD 367. Obviously, the books were regarded by most of the churches as authoritative more than two hundred years prior to that time.

6. The twenty-seven books of our New Testament were ratified by the Council of Hippo (AD 393) and the Council of Carthage (AD 397).

Here again we see the providence of God. These councils neither added nor subtracted books, but simply approved the list of twenty-seven, which had already been recognized by the early church. Given the geographical distances, the limitations of communication, and the diverse backgrounds of the churches, such agreement is remarkable.

As *Sola Scriptura!* states, "The canon, already implicitly present in the apostolic age, gradually became explicit through a number of providential factors forming and fixing it."[5] The councils of the church had no knowledge or power that was not available to Christians generally.

In answer to the questions, Who decided which books are in the Bible and when did they do it? those decisions were made as the books were written; these were decisions made by God's people, who recognized these books as authoritative. They were careful to observe all that the apostles taught and wrote, believing the apostles to be representatives of the Christ they knew in the flesh.

PROTESTANT OR CATHOLIC?

Now that we have given this brief overview of the formation of the Old and New Testament canon, we are in a better position to discuss the differences between the Protestant and Catholic views of the canon. Here is the controversial question: Does the church have authority over the canon, or does the canon have authority over the church? Rome answers unambiguously that the church gave birth to the canon, chose which books should be in the canon, and therefore has primacy over the Scriptures. And given this authority, the church has the power to adopt traditions that are not found in the Bible, and these are just as binding as the Scriptures themselves.

Vatican II in 1967 summarized the official position of the church on this issue:

> It is clear therefore, that sacred tradition, sacred Scripture and the teaching authority of the church are so linked and joined together that one cannot stand without the others, and that all together and each in his own way under the action of the Holy Spirit contribute effectively to the salvation of souls.[6]

Thus, the church promotes traditions not found in the Scriptures, and sometimes it is pointless to test these traditions with Scripture, for when a conflict arises, tradition, and not Scripture, will win the day.

Let us think through this issue:

Protestants stress that a book either does or does not have inherent authority; it is either from God or it is not. If a letter were written by Abraham Lincoln it would be authentic even if historians did not recognize it as such. And if it were not written by him, all the councils and pronouncements of men could not make it become a letter from his hand. The best we can do is to examine the letter to try to determine whether he was the author.

If a book were inspired by God, it would be authoritative even if Israel in the Old Testament and the church in the New failed to recognize it as such. And if it were not inspired, it would not matter how sincerely we believed it was of divine authorship. In other words, we must distinguish between the *authority* of a particular book and the *recognition* of that authority.

Roman Catholic theologians object to giving such primacy to the documents themselves. When Johann Eck debated Luther, he made this point, that "the Scriptures are not authentic, except by the authority of the church." In other words, the church can confer authenticity upon a book. Truth is whatever the official teachings of the church say it is. Protestants disagree.

Protestants boldly affirm that it was a fallible church that chose what we believe to be an infallible list of books that comprise our New Testament. Yes, theoretically, the church might have erred. Of course, there is no reason to believe that the church did in fact err, but error is possible for one reason: *the church is not infallible; only the Scriptures are.*

Having said that, we do not believe that the church erred for two reasons: First, there are no additional books in existence that make a serious claim for the New Testament canon. Even those canonical books whose acceptance was disputed have proved their worth, and the books that were excluded have been shown to be subbiblical. To the person who says that the church erred, I reply, "Set forth your case; give me your recommendations as to what book should be removed; and which books, if any, should be included." At that point the discussion usually ends.

Second, as already argued above, we believe that God providentially preserved His Word. He did this, however, not by making the church infallible in all of its official decisions, but by guiding His own people to recognize those books that had the stamp of divine authority.

Are you still troubled at the thought that it was a fallible church that selected what we believe to be infallible Scriptures?

You should not be surprised. *After all, it was fallible human beings who wrote the infallible Scriptures.* King David in the Old Testament and Peter in the New are examples of writers whose sins and failures are well known. Yet David wrote infallible psalms and Peter, who denied Christ, wrote two infallible epistles. Just so, a fallible church could be led of God to choose an infallible list of books.

The Catholic Church, however, insists that it has a right to its traditions because Paul exhorted the early church to follow the traditions of the apostles. "So then, brethren, stand firm and hold to the traditions which you were taught, whether by word of mouth or by letter from us (2 Thessalonians 2:15). This, it is said, gives justification for church tradition. The church, not the Scriptures, it is said, is the "pillar and ground of the truth" (1 Timothy 3:15 KJV).

However, consider the context of Paul's words in 2 Thessalonians 2:15 (quoted above). Paul had taught the believers in Thessalonica many things by word of mouth, and these doctrines were to be followed. But the essential content of these teachings is what is recorded in the Scripture. And if there were other matters Paul taught them that are not in the sacred Scriptures, we can only assume that he did not think that they were necessary to be preserved for the whole church. Paul would never have entrusted the truth he wanted the whole church to know to oral tradition. Whatever was of basic importance was written down.

The Thessalonians had evidently been misled by a forged letter, supposedly by an apostle, telling them that the day of the Lord had already come (2 Thessalonians 2:2). Paul wanted to warn them to accept only letters written in his own handwriting (3:17) and to stand fast in his teaching. So he ordered them to receive as infallible truth only that which they had heard directly from his own lips.[7] He gave no hint that there is a body of tradition that will be preserved for future generations, nor did he hint that other traditions will spring up throughout the centuries that the church is to follow.

What makes the Roman Catholic position more confusing is that the church has differing views of tradition. Some think that all binding tradition was taught by the apostles, while others believe that tradition evolves and develops through the centuries of the church. Either way, tradition, which is often in conflict with the Scriptures, is widely accepted. We see the danger in the words of Pope Pius IX given at the first Vatican Council in 1870: "I am tradition."[8] In other words, the pronouncements, whether they be the granting of special indulgences or the assumption of Mary into heaven, are all authoritative. And if, as some think, the Virgin should be proclaimed a co-redeemer with Christ, an official pronouncement would make that authoritative too!

Tradition is seldom neutral. Almost always it obscures the message of the Scriptures, often distorting its message. Human nature being what it is, the Jews also had their own body of tradition that grew up around the sacred writings. The Talmud, for example, was regarded as authoritative in its teachings. But Christ knew that anything added to the Word of God, however well intentioned, either dilutes or distorts the Word of God. He excoriated the Jewish leaders of the day, "Rightly did Isaiah prophesy of you hypocrites, as it is written: 'This people honors Me with their lips, but their heart is far away from Me. But in vain do they worship Me, teaching as doctrines the precepts of men.' Neglecting the commandment of God, you hold to the tradition of men" (Mark 7:6–8).

If this were not enough, Christ clearly said to them, "You are experts at setting aside the commandment of God in order to keep your tradition" (v. 9). Even if it does not directly contradict the Scriptures, it distorts their meaning.

If you still think that the pronouncements and traditions of the Catholic Church are infallible, there is much evidence in history to show that popes and councils have often contradicted each other and, more seriously, have contradicted the Scriptures themselves.

Here are a few examples:

- The tradition of the Roman Catholic Church teaches that the pope is the head of the church, a bishop over all bishops. But Gregory the Great, pope and saint, said that such teaching came from "a spirit of anti-Christ."[9]
- Pope Pius in 1559 said that if a person had a Bible of his own without written permission, he "cannot be absolved from his sins until he has turned in these Bibles." In contrast, Vatican II says that Christians should have easy access to Bibles.[10]

Enough has been said to show the contrast between Catholicism and Protestantism. The former believes that the canon is subject to the church; the latter believes that the church is subject to the canon.

THE BIBLE ALONE

Since the Reformation, Protestants have affirmed the Latin words *sola scriptura*, which mean "the Scriptures alone." We agree with Augustine: "In those teachings which are clearly based on the Scriptures are found *all* that concerns faith and the conduct of life" (emphasis added).

Catholic scholars have many objections to *sola scriptura;*

they insist that this teaching is not in the Bible itself! Thus Protestants, who pride themselves in believing that the Bible alone is the basis for faith and conduct, are not building their faith on the Bible alone!

The principle of *sola scriptura* was already established in the Old Testament. Indeed Moses warned, "You shall not add to the word which I am commanding you, nor take away from it, that you may keep the commandments of the Lord your God which I command you" (Deuteronomy 4:2). The reason the revelation was written down was that there might be no mistaking what God had said. Traditions of whatever variety were to be avoided.

Just as Christ appealed to Old Testament Scripture and studiously avoided the traditions of the Pharisees, so we must adhere to the teachings of the New Testament and avoid traditions that add to the Word of God. Catholic traditions function exactly like the Jewish traditions of the Talmud: the tradition becomes the standard by which the Scripture is interpreted.

Sola scriptura does not teach that everything Christ or the apostles ever did or taught is in the Bible, but rather that everything that is necessary for salvation and Christian living is found in the Bible; we need neither tradition nor further revelation. Certainly we can benefit from what others have taught about the Bible and its relevance to life. God has given teachers to the church, and we are derelict if we neglect them. But everything must be tested by the Book. We say with Isaiah, "To the law and to the testimony! If they do not speak according to this word, it is because they have no dawn" (Isaiah 8:20).

Though most Protestants would agree that tradition often clouds the clear meaning of Scripture, some disagree with *sola scriptura* for other reasons. They claim to have "words of knowledge" or "prophecies" that reveal truth from God not in the Bible. Obviously, these matters are debated, some insisting that these revelations are merely generated from within the human soul. Others think it is necessary to have additional revelations for specific guidance. Some of us are satisfied to know that the Bible, and the Bible alone, is all we need to be converted and live a holy life.

The church is built upon "the foundation of the apostles and prophets, Christ Jesus Himself being the corner stone" (Ephesians 2:20). We cannot return to the days of the early church when apostles preached and new writings were recognized as the Word of God. We are content to know that God has shared with us all we need to know.

The Scriptures are said to be "God-breathed" (2 Timothy 3:16 NIV). Neither church councils nor "words of knowledge" are said to have that authority. We return to the words of Paul: "All Scripture is inspired by God and profitable for teaching, for reproof, for correction, for training in righteousness; so that the man of God may be adequate, equipped for every good work" (2 Timothy 3:16–17).

Someone has said that the Bible is profitable for

Doctrine, that we might *know what is right*,
Reproof, that we might be able *to get right*,
Correction, that we might be able *to stay right*,
Training, that we might be able *to model what is right*.

I don't believe it is a coincidence that the book of Revelation is placed at the end of the New Testament canon. It ends with a warning that was intended to apply primarily to the book of Revelation itself, but it has wider application to all of Scripture:

> I testify to everyone who hears the words of the prophecy of this book: if anyone adds to them, God will add to him the plagues which are written in this book; and if anyone takes away from the words of the book of this prophecy, God will take away his part from the tree of life and from the holy city, which are written in this book. (REVELATION 22:18–19)

Could it be any clearer?

FOR FURTHER CONSIDERATION

Noncanonical Books

THE APOCRYPHA

If you look at the table of contents in a Roman Catholic Bible you will notice that there are additional books inserted between the Old and the New Testaments. In all, fifteen books comprise what we call the Apocrypha (the word means "hidden") though the Roman Catholic Church has accepted only eleven of these as Scripture. Because four of the eleven are combined with Old Testament books, the Douay Version of the Bible (a Roman Catholic translation) contains only seven additional books in its table of contents.

Where did these books come from?

To answer this question we must go back to the city of Alexandria in Egypt, where a group of scholars translated the Hebrew Old Testament into Greek in about the year 250 BC. This translation, known as the *Septuagint,* meaning "seventy" (allegedly this translation was completed in seventy days using seventy scholars), had a great impact on the Greek-speaking world. In fact, this translation was known and used during the time of Christ. New Testament writers showed acquaintance with it and even used it in some of their quotations.

Later editions of this translation included the apocryphal books. We cannot be sure exactly when the books appeared, but there is no evidence that they were in the Septuagint at the time of Christ. But since they were inserted in the Septuagint translation, their relative value was debated—some scholars arguing that they were Scripture, others insisting that they were subbiblical.

Those who accepted them as canonical included Irenaeus, Tertullian, and Clement of Alexandria; among those who rejected their canonicity were Athanasius, Origen, and Jerome, to name a few. In fact, when Jerome translated the Bible into Latin (the *Vulgate)* he did not want to translate the apocryphal books but was urged to do so. He made a hurried translation of them, though he kept them separate from the other books. Nevertheless, they appeared in his Latin translation.

Protestants give numerous reasons for rejecting these books as canonical. Since they describe events that took place before and during the time of Christ (the books date from about 200 BC to AD 100), they have historical value. And yet, many of us are convinced that they are not inspired Scripture. The following are some reasons for this view:

1. Though there are some allusions to the apocryphal books by New Testament writers (Hebrews 11:35; Jude 14–15), there is no direct quotation from them.[11] Neither Christ nor any New Testament writer appealed to these books to make a point or explain a doctrine. The other books, which were regarded as inspired, are often quoted with the phrase "It stands written" or its equivalent. Not so the apocryphal books.

2. Even the Roman Catholic Church made a distinction between the Apocrypha and the other books of the Old Testament prior to the Reformation. For example, Cardinal Cajetan, who opposed Luther at Augsburg in 1518, published *A Commentary on All the Authentic Historical Books of the Old Testament.* His commentary, however, did not include the Apocrypha.[12]

3. The first official council to ratify these books was the Council of Trent in 1546, only twenty-nine years after Luther posted his ninety-five theses on the door of the church in Wittenberg.[13] This council found it convenient to approve these books since they were being quoted against Luther. For example, 2 Maccabees speaks of prayers for the dead (12:46), and another book teaches salvation by works (Tobit 12:9). Even so, the council accepted only eleven of the fifteen books; we naturally would expect that these books, since they appeared together for so many centuries, would either be accepted or rejected together. But at Trent some were accepted, others bypassed.

4. The contents of the Apocrypha are subbiblical and some of the stories are clearly fanciful.[14] Bel and the Dragon, Tobit, and Judith have the earmarks of legend; the authors of these books even give hints along the way that these stories are not to be taken seriously.

5. These books contain historical errors. "It is claimed that Tobit was alive when the Assyrians conquered Israel (722 BC) as well as when Jeroboam revolted against Judah (931 BC)," which would make him at least 209 years old.[15] Yet, according to the account, he died when he was only 158 years old. Moreover, the book of Judith "speaks of Nebuchadnezzar as reigning

in Nineveh instead of Babylon (Judith 1:1)."[16] Such inaccuracies are inconsistent with the doctrine of inspiration, which teaches that inspired books are "God-breathed" and free from errors.

6. Finally, and most important, we must remember that the Apocrypha was never part of the Old Testament Hebrew canon.[17] We have already emphasized that Christ assumed that the Hebrew canon ended with the Hebrew Scriptures. The Apocrypha was written in Greek, not Hebrew, and appeared at a later time.

THE "LOST BOOKS" OF THE BIBLE

Occasionally we hear references to the so-called lost books of the Bible, books that some people think have been hidden from the general populace. In 1997, Bell publishing company of New York came out with a book by Dr. Frank Crane titled *The Lost Books of the Bible*. On the flyleaf it says that these books were not among those chosen to comprise the Bible and "were suppressed by the church, and for over fifteen hundred years were shrouded in secrecy."[18]

This is advertising hype. These books are not secret but have been known by scholars throughout the centuries, though perhaps they were not always accessible to the common man. Both Catholics and Protestants reject these books. There were something like twenty false gospels circulating in the early centuries.

Paul warned the Christians in Thessalonica not to accept any false letters sent to them under his name (2 Thessalonians 2:2). We've already learned that in order to verify the authenticity of his letter he wrote that they should verify the letter by his own handwriting (3:17).

John wrote that "there are also many other things which

Jesus did," which were not written in his book, "which if they were written in detail, I suppose that even the world itself would not contain the books that would be written" (21:25). In his gospel, John debunked a rumor circulating in the first century that he would never die (21:23–24). There were many stories about Christ that circulated in the first century that were either irrelevant or just plain false.

Dozens of these "lost" books have never vied for a position in the canon. Unlike some other books that were actually disputed, these books were recognized as legends from the beginning. These "forgotten books" are so obviously inferior that they cannot be taken seriously.

Indeed, in the preface of *The Lost Books of the Bible*, Dr. Crane admitted this point by saying that legends and apocryphal stories surround all great men such as Napoleon, Charlemagne, and Julius Caesar, so we can also expect that tales would grow up around Christ. He went on to say that Christ appealed to the "fictional minds" of His day. These writers, Crane admitted, do not pretend to write down what is strictly true, but tinge all events with their imagination. Well said.

TWO BOOKS AND WHY THEY WERE NOT INCLUDED IN THE CANON

There are, however, two books that did vie for a position in the canon which were rejected by the church. The first is the *Shepherd of Hermas*; the second is *The Gospel of Thomas*.[19]

The Shepherd of Hermas

In the *Shepherd of Hermas*, Jesus is depicted as a Shepherd giving guidance through visions to a man named Hermas, who wrote the book in Rome between AD 90–157. Hermas asks the Shepherd (Christ), "Some teachers say that there is no second repentance beyond what was granted when we were blessed in the waters of baptism and received remission for our previous sins."

Christ, who is the Shepherd, replies, "That is so; for he who has received remission for former sins ought never to sin again but live in purity . . . those who believe now, and those who shall believe in the future need no repentance of sins, since they have remission of their former sin. . . . After the Lord established this holy gift [repentance] and a man be tempted by the Devil, he has but one repentance. It is unprofitable, therefore for such a man to sin and repent repeatedly, for scarcely shall he live."

Hermas replies, "When I heard this truth, I attained life, for I know that if I do not add again to my sins I shall be saved."

Thankfully, the *Shepherd of Hermas* is not Scripture! Can you imagine a gospel that teaches that if we add to our sins we cannot be saved? Or that we have only one chance at repentance? The book continues with similar garbled ideas, part Scripture, part human insight. If you doubt whether this book should have been included in the Bible, just read it!

The Gospel of Thomas

The Gospel of Thomas is a text found in the Nag Hammadi collection of Gnostic writings, discovered in Egypt in 1945. This text, like the *Gospel of Judas* or the *Gospel of Philip*, purports to be written by an apostle, but is actually the product of Gnostic teachers who used the fame of the Apostles to give their own writings credibility.

What makes Thomas unique is that it does have many

authentic quotations of Jesus drawn from the Synoptic Gospels. But these sayings are interspersed with Gnostic teachings that stand in opposition to the teachings of the New Testament. The early church knew of the book and rejected it. Eusebius of Caesarea said it should be "cast aside as absurd and impious." Here's a sample. Jesus said, "Whoever finds the interpretation of these sayings will not experience death."

Then He continues:

> Let him who seeks continue seeking until he finds. When he finds, he will become troubled. When he becomes troubled, he will be astonished, and he will rule over all.

Want to hear more?

> When you make the two one, and when you make the inside like the outside and the outside like the inside, and the above like the below, and when you make the male and the female one and the same, so that the male not be male nor the female female; and when you fashion eyes in place of an eye, and a hand in the place of a hand and a foot in place of a foot and a likeness in place of a likeness; then you will enter [the kingdom].

Enough said.

Clearly the canon of Scripture is closed. No other books in existence have the credentials to merit inclusion; no books within the canon can be shown to be unworthy of respect as the Word of God. Surely God Himself supervised the collection process so that we can affirm that we hold in our hands His written revelation to us.

"Every word of God is tested; He is a shield to those who

take refuge in Him. *Do not add to His words or He will reprove you, and you will be proved a liar"* (Proverbs 30:5–6, emphasis added).

THE BIBLE HAS POWER TO CHANGE LIVES

Suppose you were stranded on a dimly lit street in an unsafe city neighborhood. You accidentally drive over a sharp metal object and two of your tires go flat. As you contemplate your next move, a dozen young men spill out of a nearby building and walk toward you. You can already see yourself being dragged from the car, robbed, and beaten. Or worse.

What difference would it make if you discovered that these men were on their way home from a Bible study? Such news would make even an atheist feel better. After all, one of the primary reasons we believe the Bible is the Word of God is its power. "'Is not my word like fire, declares the LORD, and like a hammer that breaks the rock in pieces?'" (Jeremiah 23:29 ESV). This does not mean that people cannot resist God's Word; they do so all the time, often with great fanfare. We've already learned that the Bible has been the target of sustained criticism and venomous attacks. Yet millions who have accepted its message gladly speak of its transforming power.

An angry young man stood at the back of a train and threw the new Bible his mother gave him as far as he could. Yet months later he returned, repentant that he had mistreated God's Book. He learned that the damaged Bible had fallen into the hands of a child who read it and was converted. Now both met as brothers in Christ; the one as a restored believer, the other as a newly converted twelve-year-old. What other book can soften the heart of an angry man and convert a child? Only the Bible.

Your respect for God can be measured by your respect for the Bible; the Bible is not God, of course, so we do not worship a book. But we regard its message as God's letter to us. When the Bible is open, God is speaking; when it is closed, He stops speaking.

And when He speaks we begin to see ourselves as we really are.

THE BIBLE:
A SWORD WITH TWO EDGES

We should not be surprised that the Word of God is compared to a sword. The Roman sword had two edges; it cut both ways. God does not use this sword to destroy His people; He uses it to wound them that He might heal them. Here we have the Word of God at work.

God gave His Word to the nation Israel, but sometimes

it did not do them any good. It did not profit them because it was not "mixed with faith." So the author of the book of Hebrews gives a warning to us, that we, too, would not fail to benefit from the good news God has provided for His people.

In this context, we have one of the strongest statements about the Bible's power. Indeed, what the Bible does, God does.

> For the word of God is living and active, sharper than any two-edged sword, piercing to the division of soul and of spirit, of joints and of marrow, and discerning the thoughts and intentions of the heart. And no creature is hidden from his sight, but all are naked and exposed to the eyes of him to whom we must give account.
> (HEBREWS 4:12–13)

Let's analyze this verse in detail.

The Word of God is "alive"; it is not just words on a page. The words of God are on the page; the message comes with God's authority. Wherever the Word of God is, the Spirit is present to make the words relevant, filled with life.

The Word of God is "active"; that is, it actually has power. We've learned that it converts the soul; we are "born again, not of corruptible seed, but of incorruptible, by the word of God, which liveth and abideth for ever" (1 Peter 1:23 KJV). When the Word of God acts, God acts.

The Word Cuts Us Open

The Bible differs from other two-edged swords in this respect, it is "sharper" than they could ever be. In Greek, the word is *tomoteros,* which comes from *temno,* which means "to cut." It is the language of surgery, the language of dissection.

The word *piercing* in Greek is *diikneomai,* which means

"to go through." The Word of God does not *divide* the soul from the spirit; rather, it *penetrates* both the soul and the spirit. In other words, it goes to the heart of what we are all about. It lays us bare.

This verse does not teach that the soul and the spirit can be separated (such a matter must be settled by an appeal to other passages of Scripture). Nor for that matter, can the "joints" and "marrow" be separated. In the human body joints and marrow are not in contact with one another, and therefore we cannot say that a sword or knife can separate them. The point of the passage is that both joints and marrow are each divided; just so the soul and spirit are each divided. The idea is that the Word of God "cuts through to the bone."

Kenneth S. Wuest quotes Vincent as saying, "The form of the expression is poetical, and signifies that the word penetrates to the inmost recesses of our spiritual being as a sword cuts through the joints and marrow of the body. The separation is not of one part from the other, but operates in each department of the spiritual nature."[1] The Word of God goes through both the soul and spirit; it goes through both the joints and the marrow. It stops at nothing until it comes to reality. In the presence of this Book, there can be no pretense.

The Word of God is also "able to judge the thoughts and intentions of the heart." To *judge* means to "sift out" and "analyze as evidence." The Word of God sits in judgment on all the activity of the soul and spirit. It separates base motives from noble ones; it distinguishes between that which is of the flesh and that which is of the spirit.

The Word judges our "thoughts," that is, the things we ponder, namely, our reflections: what we think as we drive down the expressway; what we think about other people, whether pleasant or unpleasant. Thousands of thoughts course through our minds each day. The Word of God monitors these musings moment by moment.

Not only our thoughts but also our "intentions" are judged. This refers to the origin of our thoughts; the conceptions of the past and intentions of the future are equally known. Wuest translates this last phrase as saying that the Word of God "is a sifter and analyzer of the reflections and conceptions of the heart."[2]

You and I are basically dishonest. We all have a carefully monitored defense system that prevents us from seeing ourselves as we really are. We project an image that we want others to believe, and we want to believe it ourselves.

Consider what the Word of God has to overcome if we are willing to see ourselves in a true light. Our problem is that we hide our true self from our real self; we make sure that no one knows who we really are. We live in a secret world that is carefully shielded from every prying eye. Surely not a one of us would want to have our private musings, desires, and intentions made public. It has often been said that if our thoughts were strung out for others to see, we would all flee to a desert island.

This defense system is maintained by a thousand rationalizations, a hundred different excuses for why we do what we do and think what we think. In this way, we make our life bearable; we can silence the voice of conscience by following a carefully crafted script. And we are secretly satisfied when people believe us to be better than we know we really are.

The Word of God penetrates past our psychic radar system and breaks up our defense mechanisms. It separates the good thoughts from the tainted ones; it discerns the motivations of mind and heart. It lays everything bare. Again Vincent is quoted as saying, "The Word of God has an incisive and penetrating quality. It lays bare self-delusions and moral sophistries."[3]

Paul said that he would not have known that lust was sin, except by the Law. "I would not have come to know sin except through the Law; for I would not have known about coveting if the Law had not said, 'You shall not covet'" (Romans 7:7). Apart from such a revelation he would have rationalized it, integrated it with his lifestyle, and would have seen nothing amiss in his thoughts and deeds. But the Law came, he was exposed to his sin and knew that he needed a Savior.

What we cannot do for ourselves, God's Word does for us. We cannot properly evaluate our lives without a divine standard that can set the record straight. Only the Bible can show us who we really are, rather than the person we perceive ourselves to be.

And there is more.

The Word Lays Us Bare

Imagine a corpse laid out on a table, with every sinew, every nerve, and every particle of bone and flesh laid bare. The author continues, "And there is no creature hidden from His sight, but all things are open and laid bare to the eyes of Him with whom we have to do" (Hebrews 4:13).

Let's not miss the connection between these two verses! The author of Hebrews passes easily from talking about God's *spoken* Word to God's *Incarnate* Word (Christ). Obviously, he wants us to understand that we are laid bare before the eyes of Christ. The Word of God, like an X-ray, reveals who we really are, and Christ examines the plates carefully, noting every speck.

To put it differently, we lie on God's surgical table. The Word of God has separated reality from fantasy, the right from the wrong, the pure from the tainted. In this spiritual autopsy, there is, figuratively speaking, a lump here, a diseased cell there, and a bone that has a hairline fracture. Every aspiration, every mental and emotional component is dissected, until at last reality has been revealed.

As long as we compare ourselves to others, we judge ourselves as doing quite well. It is easy to find someone who is worse than we are: just look around and you will find someone who, in your estimation, makes you feel better. But when we are spiritually laid out in God's operating room, we are answerable to Him and no one else.

Freud was right when he taught that there is within us an unconscious, a dark part of our being that we do not want to deal with; there is that penchant for self-deception, a desire to protect ourselves and to rationalize our behavior. There is some truth to the old saying that the difference between a coal miner and a therapist is simply this: the therapist goes down further, stays down longer, and comes up dirtier.

Every one of us has serpents coiled on the floor of our hearts, willing to strike when the time is right. We all know that deep down, we are capable of foolish and destructive behavior. Great men have done very sinful things. And God sees us just as we are: our potential for good, but also our potential for evil. He sees the conscious, but also the subconscious.

God shows us as much of ourselves as we are able to handle. Until confronted by Him, our standard of comparison is other people; our frame of reference is our success, our good deeds. But in the presence of God, only what He thinks matters. Finally, we are able to own up to the depressing fact that we are beyond all hope, apart from divine intervention.

Before this, we were like Saddam Hussein, who moved his chemical weapons from one fortress to another, trying to keep a step ahead of the United Nations weapons inspectors. Just so, we try to hide our sins until God uses His Word to break down our bolted doors, enter our fortresses, and reveal the hidden closets of the mind and heart. Those things we have skillfully hidden, the rationalizations that have been so meticulously rehearsed, are suddenly revealed when we are "laid bare to the eyes of Him with whom we have to do" (Hebrews 4:13).

Apart from the penetrating gaze of Scripture, we could not see the depth of God's moral standard and the extent of our departure from it. Now consider atheists who do not avail themselves of Scripture's vision into their souls, who deny God and deny the Bible as God's Word. They have no absolute basis for sin or morality, only individual preferences. In fact, they've turned everything upside down and portray religion, especially Christianity, as a great evil in the world that has caused much misery and suffering and needs to be eradicated.

"I have set out to demolish the intellectual and moral pretensions of Christianity in its most committed forms," says Sam Harris in his *Letter to a Christian Nation*.[4]

Exactly what "moral pretensions" Harris wants to demolish are not clear. Christians have an absolute moral standard set by God, given in His Word, even if they do violate those standards just like anyone else. But what about atheists? What is their moral standard, if not the Bible?

Doug Wilson poses this question to Harris: "You seem to be saying that there is a standard which Christianity does not acknowledge even though it is authoritative over Christians anyway, and that Christianity is in rebellion against this standard. . . . Who has defined this standard? You? Your friends? Is it published somewhere so I can read it? You write as though it exists. Where is it?"[5]

Harris states that the Bible counsels parents to beat children with a rod when they get out of line, and kill them when they talk back to us, that we must stone people to death for heresy, adultery, homosexuality, working on the Sabbath, worshiping graven images, practicing sorcery, and a wide variety of other "imaginary crimes."[6]

He also portrays the Bible as condoning slavery and does so by interpreting it out of context. In fact, the Bible in 1 Timothy 1:10 specifically condemns the kind of slavery that was practiced in Europe and the United States in prior centuries. Gary DeMar puts that in perspective:

> The slavery practiced in this country prior to 1860 was "man stealing," better defined as "kidnapping." Black West Africans were kidnapped, often by other Black West Africans, put on ships, brought to these shores, sold at auction, and placed in forced labor. In biblical terms, this was wrong. To maintain that this form of slavery would be reinstituted today in the name of "biblical law" is patently absurd.[7]

Here Harris betrays his ignorance of the distinctions between a culture that existed more than two millennia ago in a theocracy under certain laws specific to them and the church instituted by Jesus Christ under a new covenant. Harris is just engaging in fearmongering among those who do not understand biblical teachings in their context. He appears not to have investigated the reasoned explanations Bible scholars have given for the Scripture passages that so trouble him. His complaints come across sounding like a red herring—a diversion from the far more important truth clearly expressed in Scripture: we are accountable to God.

Mark Twain put it well when he said it's not the parts of the Bible he *doesn't* understand that bother him. It is, after all, the Bible's power to convict us of personal sin that should trouble us most.

"Many of the teachings of Christianity are, as well as being incredible and mythical, *immoral,*" writes Christopher Hitchens, displaying a similar misunderstanding of Scripture interpretation.[8] Yet atheism, which teaches that "human thoughts and emotions emerge from exceedingly complex interactions of physical entities within the brain,"[9] really has no basis for morality, other than personal preference. Even Richard Dawkins admits, "We can all agree that science's entitlement to advise us on moral values is problematic, to say the least."[10]

Of course, even Christians stand in continual need of conforming their thoughts and behavior to God's moral direction in Scripture. Dr. Alan Redpath, pastor of Moody Church during the 1960s, often preached on the need for submission to Christ and urged his congregation to have the faith to receive the fullness of the Holy Spirit. Often he chided the congregation (as most preachers do) to be more holy, more devoted, and more sanctified.

Years later, he had a stroke, and during that period of recovery sins revealed themselves; sins that he thought were no longer a part of his life. "Sinful thoughts, temptation to impurity, bad language were all the shattering experiences of those days." His despair was so great he wished that he could die and go to heaven. But God seemed to say to him, "I want to replace you with Myself, if you will only allow Me to be God in you, and admit that you are a complete failure, and that *the only good thing about Alan Redpath is Jesus.*" Long after his recovery I invited him to return to The

Moody Church and when he preached here, he, in effect, asked the congregation to forgive him for preaching sermons he had not lived up to!

I also plead guilty. I've preached my share of sermons that I have not lived up to. Yes, I am in the process of learning that "the only good thing about Erwin Lutzer is Jesus Christ." I hope to learn that before I have a stroke or am told that I have terminal cancer. We are probably never more holy than when we have finally agreed with Paul, "that nothing good dwells in me, that is, in my flesh" (Romans 7:18).

The reason Pastor Redpath was aware of his sins, and the reason the rest of us are aware of ours, is because the Word does its work in our lives. Apart from the Word, we would justify ourselves and, standing next to others, would die congratulating ourselves on how well we had lived.

You never talked about yourself at all! I congratulated myself as I left a luncheon this week. I had spent the time asking questions about others, asking about their lives, their vocations, and their problems. While I was reflecting on my humility, I was reminded of the verse in Proverbs, "These six things doth the Lord hate: yea, seven are an abomination unto him: a proud look . . ." (Proverbs 6:16–17 KJV). I laughed when I realized how proud I was of my humility!

Trivial, right? Yes, trivial, until we see God!

The Word Heals Us

Our natural tendency is to run from someone who knows too much about us. But although God knows everything there is to know about us, there is no place to hide. But God does not leave us on the operating table unattended. Through His Word He shows us what He sees, not that we might run *from* Him, but that we might run *to* Him. He wants us to flee to His grace and forgiveness.

Following this passage about God's knowledge of us, the author of Hebrews wrote, "Therefore let us draw near with confidence to the throne of grace, so that we may receive mercy and find grace to help in time of need" (4:16). Those who know how bad off they are have a better chance of being restored than those who see their infractions as minor matters.

Gordius tied a knot with such complexity and tightness that no one could untie it. But Alexander came, too wise to try to untie it, and cut it with his sword. God's sword is just as able to extricate us from the knots made by our own sin as it is from knots that others have tied for us. But first we must be convinced that our situation is beyond hope, apart from divine grace.

Our problem is that we want vitamins, not a knife; we want chemotherapy rather than corrective surgery. We want the healing without the incision, the joy without the sorrow. But God gives us both. For the more thorough our repentance, the greater the infusion of grace. The more helpless we see ourselves to be, the more helpful God becomes. Surgery precedes recovery.

Accept this word of comfort. "See now that I, I am He, and there is no god beside Me; it is I who put to death and give life. I have wounds, and it is I who heal, and there is no one who can deliver from My hand" (Deuteronomy 32:39). God wounds that He might heal; He cuts us open that He might sew us together. Speaking of Israel we read, "He sent His word and healed them, and delivered them from their destructions" (Psalm 107:20). His Word did the work.

"He heals the brokenhearted and binds up their wounds" (Psalm 147:3). The promises of God are the Band-Aids that God uses to heal the wounds of the soul.

God does this through revelation: we see ourselves because we see God.

John Wesley demonstrated an attitude toward God's Word worth emulating:

> I am a creature of a day, passing through life as an arrow through the air . . . a few months hence, I am no more seen, I drop into an unchangeable eternity! I want to know one thing: the way to heaven. God Himself has condescended to teach the way; He has written it down in a book. O give me that book—*at any price give me that book!*

When we let the Word reign in our lives, we are letting God reign in our lives. "For You have magnified Your word according to all Your name" (Psalm 138:2).

We should not be surprised to learn that the Bible has some of the same characteristics as God. Sometimes it is described as doing what God does, or even having some of His attributes.

God is light, and the Bible is light too. "Your word is a lamp to my feet and a light to my path" (Psalm 119:105). As a child, the light of my father's lantern guided us as we walked along the path from the house to the barn and from there to the garage or pasture. We had enough light for a few steps and then a few more, and so it went. God's Word is like that, giving us the guidance we need for the moment. The Ten Commandments are like lanterns that guard us from falling into the ditch. And the other precepts and promises help us experience God's presence and specific instruction.

Other similarities between God and the Bible are found in Psalm 19. There we see the unity between God's book of nature and God's book of words. Nature tells us of God's glory and power; but it tells us nothing of His love and mercy. In fact, nature is fallen; therefore in some respects it is quite unlike God.

The Scriptures are more accurate than nature can ever be, not only because language is more precise, but also because they do not err. The claims David makes for the Bible are astounding. If wrong, the Bible is the world's most dangerous forgery; if right, we can rejoice that we have a word from God to guide us along the paths of life.

SIMILARITIES BETWEEN THE BIBLE AND GOD

In Psalm 19 there are six adjectives that apply to the Bible, but they also apply to God. Read them in your own Bible and underline each one. You'll be surprised at these lofty claims that inspire the confidence that the Bible is indeed God's Book.

Perfection

"The law of the Lord is perfect, restoring the soul" (v. 7). Perfection is a characteristic of God; He sets the standard for what perfection really is. Only a book with such power can "restore the soul." The Bible probes into that inward part of us that no one sees; it brings us back to our senses—and back to our God.

In fact, the Word of God not only restores us, but it saves us. When God converts us, it is through the power of His Word: "For you have been born again not of seed which is perishable but imperishable, that is, through the living and enduring word of God. For, 'All flesh is like grass, and all its glory like the flower of grass. The grass withers, and the flower falls off, but the word of the Lord endures forever'"

(1 Peter 1:23–25). James agrees: "In the exercise of His will He brought us forth by the word of truth, so that we would be a kind of first fruits among His creatures" (James 1:18).

The Spirit of God, using the Word of God, grants us a miracle from God. Almost always when people tell about how they came to saving faith in Christ, they will quote a verse of Scripture that caused them to see the truth, or else they will refer to the message of the gospel in their own words. Either way, the *Word* of God, conveying the *will* of God, did the *work* of God.

Faithfulness

"The testimony of the Lord is sure, making wise the simple" (v. 7). That word *sure* means faithful, dependable, and certain. As a result of God's steadfastness, we are given direction in life.

Today we use the word *simple* in a derogatory sense, but it means "to be easily led astray." All of us are easily led astray; we can fall fast and far. Staying close to the Word keeps us from those foolish decisions. God is faithful; His word is faithful. Count on it.

Righteousness

"The precepts of the Lord are right, rejoicing the heart" (v. 8). The Hebrew word for *right* has the same root as *righteousness,* which is, of course, one of God's most prominent attributes. We can be thankful that the Scriptures are also right, giving us the standard by which conduct must be judged. Looked at correctly, they "rejoice the heart."

Purity

"The commandment of the Lord is pure, enlightening the eyes" (v. 8). Like the God whom they reflect, the Scriptures are *pure,* free from the contamination of error. As a result they illuminate our true condition and show us the right path. Here is wisdom and understanding.

Today many people are seeking enlightenment through the "transformation of consciousness" that comes through drugs or transcendental meditation. Unfortunately, these "insights" are often contradictory and even demonic. The good news is that we need not try to force our way into the metaphysical world in a quest for answers. God has given us His Word, which, properly understood, brings all the enlightenment we need.

Cleanness

"The fear of the Lord is clean, enduring forever" (v. 9). Just because the words *Scripture, commandment,* or *law* do not occur in this phrase, we should not think that David was no longer talking about God's Book. Clearly the word *fear* is a synonym for the law of God. One of the purposes of the Law is "so they may learn to *fear* Me all the days they live on the earth, and that they may teach their children" (Deuteronomy 4:10).

The law of God is *clean,* that is, unmixed with error; it does not misrepresent God. Those who follow its precepts honor that which endures forever. Here an eternal perspective is revealed.

Truth

"The judgments of the Lord are true; they are righteous altogether" (v. 9). God is the standard of truth by which all matters must be judged. And that standard is reflected in the law of God.

Because David's Bible was the Law of Moses and a few other historical books, we might wonder how reading and meditating on these writings could bless him. He lived long before the prophets told of both the judgment and the mercy of God; he lived many centuries before the New Testament was written with its lofty truths and promises.

Yet, despite these limitations, he said of God's precepts, "They are more desirable than gold, yes, than much fine gold; sweeter also than honey and the drippings of the honeycomb. Moreover, by them Your servant is warned; in keeping them there is great reward" (vv. 10–11).

And so long before God displayed His grace in the coming of Christ, long before the Holy Spirit was sent to the church for a new ministry, long before the promises of Romans 8 were penned, David found the law of God to be sweet and the keeping of God's law brimming with "great reward."

Try telling investors on Wall Street that you have found the Bible to be more precious than fine gold! Given the confusion of values that permeates our culture, these words strike us as oddly out of step with the times. But the fact remains that those who love the law of God, though they love nothing else, are better off than those who have everything else, but ignore the law of God.

David concluded the psalm by applying the law to himself, and therefore to us. "Who can discern his errors? Acquit me of hidden faults. Also keep back Your servant from presumptuous sins; let them not rule over me; then I will be blameless, and I shall be acquitted of great transgression. Let the words of my mouth and the meditation of my heart be acceptable in Your sight, O Lord, my rock and my Redeemer" (vv. 12–14).

In the Bible we are confronted by a God who is so unlike us that we fall on our knees, accepting His forgiveness and grace. We invite a rigorous examination. We are at once smitten and comforted; we are cut open and healed. David asked: "Who can discern his errors?" (v. 12). Not a one of us knows the depth of sin in our heart. But, as the saying goes, the God who knows us the best, loves us the most.

"Also keep back Your servant from presumptuous sins; let them not rule over me" (v. 13). David prayed that he might not commit those deliberate sins, those sins that most assuredly would destroy him. Only through meditation in the Scriptures do we know what those sins are and how they can be avoided. All of this instruction is not only for our good, but also for God's glory.

IS CHRISTIANITY EVIL AND ATHEISM MORAL?

Some atheists attempt to portray religion in general and God in particular in a very different light—as evil. They do so by selectively pointing out evils done in the name of religion, ignoring all the good, and by distorting the very character of God. And they assert the moral goodness of atheism, overlooking massive evidence to the contrary. To them the world would be a much better place without religion. Yet the evidence shows otherwise, especially with respect to Christianity.

The evils that atheists tend to bring up like the Inquisition and the Crusades had little to do with biblical Christianity and much to do with attempting to stop Muslim invaders from taking control of the Holy Land and Europe. These endeavors pale in comparison with the slaughter of millions under the atheistic regimes of Stalin, Lenin, Hitler, Ceausescu, and Pol Pot.

Contrast those with the influence for good that Christianity has engendered in all areas of life: for basic human freedoms; protection of children and the unborn; women's rights; the sanctity of marriage and sex; advances in health care, education, literature, the arts and sciences; institutions of charity and justice; and the abolition of slavery, as Alvin J. Schmidt documents in his book *How Christianity Changed the World.*

Much of the mores of Western culture we may take for granted did not exist in Greco-Roman cultures and other pagan societies in various parts of the world, Schmidt points out. Practices like infanticide, child abandonment, human sacrifice, and suicide were condoned and often advocated in those cultures.[11]

Sexual promiscuity and depravity pervaded pagan Roman culture. Adultery and fornication were common, and marital faithfulness disappeared. Early Greek and Roman men engaged unashamedly in sex with boys aged twelve to sixteen. A double standard prevailed with respect to adultery, favoring men.[12]

Christians condemned these practices and transformed their cultures. Even our post-Christian culture in America and Europe still mostly abhors such practices, often not realizing Christianity's influence in their thinking that human life is sacred.

Christianity has vastly elevated the status of women in the Western world today, Schmidt says, as compared to the low status they had in ancient pagan cultures and in some contemporary cultures. The Bible's command to husbands, "Love your wives, just as Christ also loved the church and gave himself up for her" (Ephesians 5:25) is a radical idea in cultures that devalue women and regard them as little more than their husbands' property.

> The liberty and justice that are enjoyed by humans in Western societies and in some non-Western countries are increasingly seen as the projects of a benevolent, secular government that is the provider of all things. There seems to be no awareness that the liberties and rights that are currently operative in free societies of the West are to a great degree the result of Christianity's influence. The architects of civic freedom and justice—men like St. Ambrose, Stephen Langton, John Locke, Baron de Montesquieu, Thomas Jefferson, and James Madison—all drew extensively from the Christian perspective regarding humanity's God-given freedoms, which for most of human history had never really been implemented.[13]

In an extensive study of philanthropy, Arthur Brooks found that religious conservatives give more of their money and time by far than do secular liberals, who tend to see charity as the government's role.[14]

What has atheism done for the poor, the sick, the disenfranchised, those in prison or enslaved, and the victims of injustice when compared with what Christian organizations and individual Christians have been doing and continue to do in these areas?

Consider the basic human freedoms of religion and expression. These do not exist under Islamic or atheistic regimes, which force their beliefs on others. Tolerance is a Judeo-Christian value that allows expression of opposing views. Atheism repeatedly shows its intolerance of Christian views in academia and the public square. Harris proclaims that particular sort of intolerance as the very purpose of his book: "The primary purpose of this book is to arm secularists in our society, who believe that religion should be kept out of public policy, against their opponents on the Christian

Right."[15] What irony—and hypocrisy—that he would deny Christians the freedom of expression he himself enjoys in a nation founded on biblical values.

The Word of God is to the soul what food is to the body. And the Bible gives us a whole meal. It is milk and meat; it is bread and, for dessert, it gives us honey. The Bible is everything we need for "soul maintenance."

Charles Spurgeon, an English nineteenth-century preacher, wrote:

> Why, the Book has wrestled with me; the Book has smitten me; the Book has comforted me; the Book has smiled on me; the Book has frowned on me; the Book has clasped my hand; the Book has warmed my heart. The Book weeps with me, and sings with me; it whispers to me, and it preaches to me; it maps my way, and holds up my goings; it is the Young Man's Best Companion, and is still my morning and evening Chaplain.[16]

Remember the bottom line: The Bible reflects the character of God. Therefore the descriptions it uses to describe itself are the descriptions that also apply to the Almighty Himself.

FOR FURTHER CONSIDERATION

The Path to Personal Transformation

God gave a promise to Joshua: "This book of the law shall not depart from your mouth, but you shall meditate on it day and night, so that you may be careful to do according to all that is written in it; for then you will make your way prosperous, and then you will have success" (Joshua 1:8).

Here is another promise: The man who is blessed does not accept the counsel of the wicked, "but his delight is in the law of the Lord, and in His law he meditates day and night. He will be like a tree firmly planted by streams of water, which yields its fruit in its season and its leaf does not wither; and in whatever he does, he prospers" (Psalm 1:2–3).

If we want to experience the powerful effects of the Scriptures on our lives, we must learn to meditate on their teachings and promises. Several blessings will follow. First, there is *stability*. "He shall be like a tree planted by the rivers of water" (v. 3 KJV). As you visualize this tree, notice that it has signs of life in the midst of drought. The same Word of God that *gives* believers life, now *sustains* that life.

Horticulturists tell us that the root system beneath the ground is just as large as the tree above the ground. A tree that has its roots firmly planted beside a stream can withstand the winds of adversity. People marvel that the tree can survive in a desert, but it is because it is close to the oasis.

When the wife of a friend of mine was dying of cancer, he accepted this tragedy with a sense of calm and peace. I asked him how he was able to cope with the anger and anxiety that usually accompanied such difficult situations. He replied, "I read the Bible to my wife, chapter after chapter; then we bought the New Testament on tape, so that the Word of God was heard constantly in our home. The Scriptures pushed the bitterness and anxiety from our hearts and gave us peace." That is stability.

Second, there is *fruitfulness*. This is a tree that "yields its fruit in its season" (v. 3). Fruit is the expression of the inner nature. You don't have to be an expert to recognize an orange tree; just look for oranges. The fruit that God grows in our lives is the expression of His inner nature: "love, joy, peace, patience, kindness, goodness, faithfulness, gentleness, self-control" (Galatians 5:22–23). Fruit cannot be manufactured; it can only be grown.

Growth needs both sunshine and darkness. During the day the trees derive energy from the sun; at night that energy is conserved and the tree is given rest. Just so, we need sunshine and darkness; encouragement as well as pain. Jesus said that we can bear fruit that "remains." That is, we can bear fruit that will last for an eternity.

Of course, pruning is necessary for such fruit. The sharp knife that cuts back the twigs and leaves causes the energy to go into the branch. Remember, God's first priority is not our happiness, but our growth.

Even when the drought comes, the tree planted close to the stream can survive. When we are between jobs, when we have been unjustly fired, when our expectations are dashed to the ground—even then our leaves can be green.

How can we achieve such a life of stability? Two words come to mind when I think of meditation. The first word is *mull*, which means to ponder or to think. When you read a passage from the Bible you should ask: What does this text teach me about God? What does it tell me to do? What thought can I take with me for the day? Unless we ask the text some questions, we might put our Bible down and not know what we have read.

In Europe a couple bought a jewelry box they were told would glow all night. But when they set it on their dresser for the night, it did not glow at all. They found a friend who could read the French and discovered that the instructions read, "Put me in the sunlight during the day and I will glow all night."

Second, we must *memorize* the Scriptures. We think we cannot memorize the Scriptures, but of course we can! If I offered you a hundred dollars for every verse you learned, you would discover that you could memorize quite quickly. God's promise is not for the one hundred dollars, but for something far better, namely, a stable, fruitful life.

If you struggle with anxiety, memorize verses that assure believers of God's peace. If your problem is moral impurity, memorize verses about a clean heart. If you struggle with guilt, memorize verses that assure us of God's forgiveness. The promise is that those who meditate will be blessed. "With my whole heart I seek you; let me not wander from your commandments! I have stored up your word in my heart, that I might not sin against you" (Psalm 119:10–11 ESV).

Holy Bible, book divine,
Precious treasure, thou art mine;
Mine to tell me whence I came;
Mine to teach me what I am; . . .
Mine to tell of joys to come,
And the rebel sinner's doom;
O thou holy book divine,
Precious treasure, thou art mine.
—JOHN BURTON

FOR DOUBTERS
ONLY

Once I spoke to a man who told me that he was not convinced that the Bible was the Word of God, though he believed "most of it." He could accept parts of the Bible, but could not believe some of the miracles; he doubted whether the authors of Scripture were truly freed of their cultural limitations when they condemned homosexuality and taught that creation took place in six days. If he had to believe the Bible was verbally inspired from cover to cover, he said he could "never become a Christian."

I gave him this advice: Begin reading the New Testament, particularly the book of John, a chapter a day. "And, before you open the Bible," I said, "pray and ask God to show you whether or not this is the truth."

It's too soon to know whether he will become a Christian, but my point was simply that a person does not have to accept the Bible as the inerrant Word of God before he or she chooses to believe on Christ. This man, like many others, was brought up in religious schools and a strict home. Part of his problem was that he was rebelling against an oppressive kind of Christianity, from which he was now "liberated." I encouraged him to take a fresh look at the Bible, free of the stereotypes that played such a big part in his formative years.

Doubts can be good if they lead us to seek the truth at any cost. Many strong believers confess that they were, at one time, very weak in the faith. Some have come to Christ trembling "with many a conflict, many a doubt," as the hymn puts it. Today, they have grown in their confidence that Christ is who He claimed to be and that their lives are secure in God's hands. They have also come to believe in the complete trustworthiness of the Bible.

"Unlike other religious texts, the Bible gives us the good, the bad, and the ugly of its heroes: Abraham, Jacob, David, and Peter among them," writes Stan Guthrie. "Further, Scripture's message rings true. It has been said that human depravity is the only religious doctrine empirically verified on a daily basis. And the Bible's gracious solution to our predicament, Christ's atoning death on the Cross, uniquely emphasizes what God has done, not what we must do, for our rescue."[1]

Many people are converted before they understand the doctrine of the inerrancy of Scripture. As I have emphasized before, once the Holy Spirit grants a person the gift of repentance and he or she is "born again," belief in the infallibility of the Bible usually follows quite naturally. If God can save me, He can, most assuredly, do the miracles recorded in the pages of Scripture.

Factual doubts are doubts that are of the intellectual variety. Just like my friend, some people have genuine questions about whether the Bible can be true.

Volitional doubt is more difficult. It is a choice to not believe, most probably for moral reasons. In this case the intellectual doubts are often a smoke screen for a fundamental unwillingness to investigate the Scriptures seriously.

Emotional doubts describe those people who are often plagued with anxiety, depression, or guilt. They seem to have lost all hope of finding peace. Often such people wish to believe, but their emotional equilibrium does not give them the freedom to resolve the question of faith and evidence. We have probably all experienced that kind of doubt.

C. S. Lewis wrote, "Our faith in Christ wavers not so much when real arguments come against it as when it *looks* improbable—when the whole world takes on that desolate *look* which really tells us much more about the state of our passions and even our digestion than about reality."[2]

If you find yourself wanting to believe but unable to do so, let me stress the need to look to Christ. We can do no better than to renew our confidence in Him as the one and only Savior; the One who will not deceive us.

J. B. Phillips, a London pastor, known to many for his modern-language translation of the New Testament, wrote a book titled *Ring of Truth*. In it he told what happened to him when he discovered Christ to be all that he needed. His words describe both the doubts and discoveries of someone who was searching for truth, for reality.

What happened to me as progressed, was that the figure of Jesus emerged more and more clearly, and in a way unexpectedly. Of course, I had a deep respect, indeed a great reverence for the conventional Jesus Christ whom the church worshipped. But I was not at all prepared for the unconventional man revealed in these terse Gospels: this was no puppet-hero built out of the imaginations of adoring followers. This man Jesus, so briefly described, rang true, sometimes alarmingly true. I began to see why the religious Establishment of those days wanted to get rid of him at all costs. *He was sudden death to pride, pomposity and pretense.* (emphasis added)[3]

Of course, the verbal inspiration of the Bible is important, for the integrity of Scripture lies at the heart of Bible doctrine. But a skeptic need not begin there; he can study Christ, can read of Him with an open mind. And Christ will be *sudden death to pride, pomposity, and pretense.*

Jesus answered, "If I glorify Myself, My glory is nothing; it is My Father who glorifies Me, of whom you say, 'He is our God'; and you have not come to know Him, but I know Him; and if I say that I do not know Him, I will be a liar like you, but I do know Him and keep His word. Your Father Abraham rejoiced to see My day, and he saw it and was glad."

So the Jews said to Him, "You are not yet fifty years old, and have You seen Abraham?"

Jesus said to them, "Truly, truly, I say to you, before Abraham was born, I am." (JOHN 8:54–58)

Where else can one hear words like these?

NOTES

Preface

1. Nancy Pearcey, *Total Truth* (Wheaton, IL: Crossway, 2005), 20–21.
2. Ibid., 22.
3. Lynn Andriani, "The Anti-Religion Books," *Publishers Weekly*, June 4, 2007.
4. Woody Allen, "Adrift Alone in the Cosmos," *New York Times*, August 10, 1979.
5. Francis A. Schaeffer, *The Great Evangelical Disaster* (Westchester, IL: Crossway, 1984), 37.
6. Francis A. Schaeffer, *No Final Conflict* (Downers Grove, IL: InterVarsity, 1979), 119.

Introduction: Waiting to Hear God Speak

1. Alister McGrath and Joanna Collicutt McGrath, *The Dawkins Delusion* (Downer's Grove, IL: InterVarsity, 2007), 12.

2. Sam Harris, *Letter to a Christian Nation* (New York: Alfred A. Knopf, 2006), viii.
3. Ludwig Wittgenstein, "Wittgenstein's Lecture on Ethics," *Philosophical Review* 74 (1965): 7.
4. Ravi Zacharias, *The End of Reason* (Grand Rapids: Zondervan, 2008), 14–15, 24, 26.
5. Quoted in John Ankerberg and John Weldon, *Ready with an Answer* (Eugene, OR: Harvest House, 1997), 67.
6. Harris, *Letter to a Christian Nation*, 79.
7. Richard Dawkins, *The God Delusion* (New York: Houghton Mifflin, 2006), 36.
8. Victor J. Stenger, *God: The Failed Hypothesis: How Science Shows That God Does Not Exist* (Amherst, NY: Prometheus, 2007).
9. Norman Geisler and Frank Turek, *I Don't Have Enough Faith to Be an Atheist* (Wheaton, IL: Crossway, 2004), 25.
10. J. I. Packer, Introduction to *Knowing Scripture*, by R. C. Sproul (Downers Grove, IL: InterVarsity, 1979), 9.
11. Dawkins, *The God Delusion*, 92–93.
12. Bernard Ramm, *Protestant Christian Evidences* (Chicago: Moody, 1953), 230–31.
13. Josh McDowell, *The New Evidence That Demands a Verdict*, rev. ed. (Nashville: Thomas Nelson, 1999), 9, 34.
14. Ramm, *Protestant Christian Evidences*, 231.
15. Deborah Fleck, "Center for the Study of New Testament Manuscripts Working to Preserve Ancient Pieces," *The Dallas Morning News*, March 8, 2008.
16. This quotation, widely reprinted, has been attributed to Robert Cleaver Chapman (1803–1902).

Reason One: The Bible Claims to Be God's Word

1. Victor J. Stenger, *God: The Failed Hypothesis: How Science Shows That God Does Not Exist* (Amherst, NY: Prometheus, 2007), 171.
2. Frank E. Gaebelein, "The Unity of the Bible," in *Revelation and the Bible*, ed. Carl F. Henry (Grand Rapids: Baker, 1958), 394.
3. Floyd E. Hamilton, *The Basis of Christian Faith* (New York: Harper & Row, 1946), 156.
4. F. F. Bruce, *The Books and the Parchments* (New York: Revell, 1963), 88.
5. L. Gaussen, *Theopneustia* (Kansas City, MO: Gospel Union, 1912), 38.

Reason Two: History Confirms the Bible's Reliability

1. *Time*, 18 December 1995, 67.
2. Ibid., 68.
3. Ibid., 70.
4. *The New American Standard Open Bible*, quoted in John Ankerberg and John Weldon, *Ready with an Answer* (Eugene, OR: Harvest House, 1997), 260.

5. Ankerberg and Weldon, *Ready with an Answer*, 262.

6. Ibid., 269.

7. Floyd E. Hamilton, *The Basis of Christian Faith* (New York: Harper & Row, 1946), 172.

8. Clifford A. Wilson, *Rocks, Relics and Biblical Reliability* (Grand Rapids: Zondervan, 1977), 23.

9. Robert T. Boyd, *Boyd's Handbook of Practical Apologetics* (Grand Rapids: Kregel, 1997), 143.

10. Ibid., 145.

11. Hamilton, *The Basics of the Christian Faith*, 175–77.

12. "Score One for the Bible," *Time*, March 5, 1990, 59.

13. "Scholars Dismiss Jesus Documentary," *CBS News*, February 26, 2007, http://www.cbsnews.com/stories/2007/02/26/world/main2514360.shtml.

14. Boyd, *Boyd's Handbook of Practical Apologetics*, 185–86.

15. John Warwick Montgomery, *History and Christianity* (Minneapolis: Bethany, 1965), 25–35. This book is a vigorous and convincing presentation of the reliability of the New Testament portrait of Christ.

16. Ibid., 26–27.

17. Ibid., 28.

18. Josephus, *The Essential Writings*, ed. Paul Maier (Grand Rapids: Kregel, 1988), 264.

19. Bernard Ramm, *Protestant Christian Evidences* (Chicago: Moody, 1957), 232–33.

20. Norman L. Geisler and William E. Nix, *A General Introduction to the Bible*, rev. and exp. ed. (Chicago: Moody, 1986), 367.

21. Norman L. Geisler and William E. Nix, *A General Introduction to the Bible* (Chicago: Moody, 1968), 263.

22. Millar Burrows, *The Dead Sea Scrolls* (New York: Viking, 1958), 304; quoted in Geisler and Nix, *General Introduction to the Bible* (1986), 367.

23. Boyd, *Boyd's Handbook of Practical Apologetics*, 175–77.

24. Geisler and Nix, *A General Introduction to the Bible* (1968), 263.

Reason Three: Bible Prophecies Prove Its Truthfulness

1. Ray Comfort, *The Secrets of Nostradamus Exposed* (Bellflower, CA: Living Waters, 1996), 47.

2. Ibid., 49.

3. Ibid., 55.

4. John Ankerberg and John Weldon, *Ready with an Answer* (Eugene, OR: Harvest House, 1997), 248.

5. Ibid., 248.

6. Ibid., 223–24.

7. Sam Harris, *Letter to a Christian Nation* (New York: Alfred A. Knopf, 2006), 57.

8. Doug Wilson, *Letter from a Christian Citizen* (Powder Springs, GA: American Vision, 2007), 67–68.

9. Michael Drosnin, *The Bible Code* (New York: Simon & Schuster, 1997), 1.

10. Jeffrey B. Satinover, "Divine Authorship," *The Bible Review*, October 1995: 44.

11. Shlomo Sternberg, "Snake Oil for Sale," *The Bible Review*, August 1997: 24–25.

12. Randall Ingermanson, *Who Wrote the Bible Code: A Physicist Probes the Current Controversy* (Colorado Springs: WaterBrook, 1999).

13. Jim Myers, "Do Bible Codes Predict the Future?" *The Informed Believer* 8, no. 7:2.

Reason Four: Christ Affirmed the Bible's Authority and Truth

1. Quoted in "The Gospel Truth?" *Time*, April 8, 1996, 54.

2. Ibid.

3. Ibid., 55.

4. Erwin W. Lutzer, *Christ Among Other gods* (Chicago: Moody, 1994), 94–95. This book discusses the authority of Christ in further detail.

5. John W. Wenham, *Christ and the Bible* (Grand Rapids: Baker, 1994), 14.

6. Ibid., 21.

7. Ibid., 22.

8. Ibid., 28.

9. Edward J. Young, *Thy Word Is Truth* (Grand Rapids: Eerdmans, 1957), 55.

10. John Warwick Montgomery, *History and Christianity* (Minneapolis: Bethany, 1965).

11. Quoted in Montgomery, *History and Christianity*, 67–68.

12. Ibid., 72.

13. "Richard Dawkins: You Ask the Questions Special," *The Independent*, December 4, 2006.

14. Richard Dawkins, *The God Delusion* (New York: Houghton Mifflin, 2006), 92.

15. Regis Nicoll, "Why the Heathen Rage," www.breakpoint.org/listingarticle.asp?ID=7273.

16. Bruce E. Hunsberger and Bob Altemeyer, *Atheists: A Groundbreaking Study of America's Unbelievers* (Amherst, NY: Prometheus, 2006), 107.

17. Paul Enns, *The Moody Handbook of Theology*, rev. and exp. (Chicago: Moody, 2008), 627.

18. Wolfhart Pannenberg, in a conversation with Ron Sider, *Prism Magazine*, March/April, 1997.

19. John Stott, *Why I Am a Christian* (Downers Grove, IL: InterVarsity, 2003), 34–35, 36.

20. Ravi Zacharias, *The End of Reason* (Grand Rapids: Zondervan, 2008), 26.

Reason Five: Science Supports Biblical Creation

1. Henry M. Morris, *The Genesis Record* (Grand Rapids: Baker, 1976), 38.
2. William Lane Craig, *Reasonable Faith: Christian Truth and Apologetics*, 3rd ed. (Wheaton, IL: Crossway, 2008), 114.
3. Daniel Dennett, *Breaking the Spell: Religion as a Natural Phenomenon* (New York: Viking, 2006), 242, quoted in ibid.
4. Victor J. Stenger, *God: The Failed Hypothesis: How Science Shows That God Does Not Exist* (Amherst, NY: Prometheus, 2007), 175.
5. Simon Mitton and Jacqueline Mitton, *The Young Oxford Book of Astronomy* (New York: Oxford, 1995), 146.
6. Ibid.
7. Fred Heeren, *Show Me God* (Wheeling, IL: Searchlight, 1995), 187. This helpful book shows that science consistently points to an intelligent Creator. It cites many scientific authorities, both Christian and atheist, who confirm that the design of the universe cannot be accounted for within a naturalistic framework.
8. *The Chicago Tribune*, November 15, 1997.
9. Edward P. Tyron, "What Made the World?" *New Scientist* 101 (March 8, 1984): 14.
10. Heeren, *Show Me God*, 82.
11. Ibid.
12. Ibid., 113.
13. Rodney Stark, *The Victory of Reason: How Christianity Led to Freedom, Capitalism, and Western Success* (New York, Random House, 2005).
14. Alister McGrath and Joanna Collicutt McGrath, *The Dawkins Delusion* (Downer's Grove, IL: InterVarsity, 2007), 51.
15. Ibid., 44.
16. Ibid., 45.
17. Ibid., 34–35.
18. Sam Harris, *Letter to a Christian Nation* (New York: Alfred A. Knopf, 2006), 71.
19. Ibid., 68.
20. Ibid., 70.
21. McGrath and McGrath. *The Dawkins Delusion*, 11.
22. Nancy Pearcey, *Total Truth* (Wheaton, IL: Crossway, 2005), 42.
23. Guillermo Gonzalez, "Is the Earth Special? Re-examining the Copernican Principle" (unpublished paper, n.d.). Dr. Gonzalez is a research astronomer at the University of Washington.
24. Ibid.
25. *The World Book Encyclopedia*, 1972 ed., s.v. "Moon."
26. Mitton and Mitton, *The Young Oxford Book of Astronomy*, 98.
27. Ibid., 32.
28. Robert Jastrow, *The Intellectuals Speak Out about God* (Lake Bluff, IL: Regnery Gateway, 1984), 21.

29. Hereen, *Show Me God*, 202.
30. Ibid.
31. Ibid., 201.
32. Pearcey, *Total Truth*, 11.
33. Hereen, *Show Me God*, 110.
34. D. M. S. Watson, *Nature* (1929), quoted in Duane Gish, *Evolution? The Fossils Say No!* (San Diego: Creation Life, 1973), 24.
35. Phillip E. Johnson, *Darwin on Trial* (Downers Grove, IL: InterVarsity, 1993).
36. Quoted in John Ankerberg and John Weldon, *Darwin's Leap of Faith* (Eugene, OR: Harvest House, 1998), 11.
37. Phillip E. Johnson, "The Unraveling of Scientific Materialism," *First Things*, no. 71 (November 1997): 23.
38. Walter T. Brown, *In the Beginning* (Naperville, IL: ICR, Midwest Center, 1981), 3.
39. Michael Behe, *Darwin's Black Box: The Biochemical Challenge to Evolution* (New York: Free Press, 1997), 41.
40. John Stott, *Why I Am a Christian* (Downers Grove, IL: InterVarsity, 2003), 70.
41. Ibid., 72.

Reason Six: God's People, by His Providence, Recognized the Canon

1. Stephen K. Ray, *Crossing the Tiber* (San Francisco: Ignatius, 1997), 54.
2. Ibid., 55.
3. Norman L. Geisler and William E. Nix, *A General Introduction to the Bible*, rev. and exp. ed. (Chicago: Moody, 1986), 420, 430.
4. Ibid., 430.
5. *Sola Scriptura! The Protestant Position on the Bible*, ed. Don Kistler (Morgan, PA: Soli Deo Gloria Publications, 1995), 19.
6. Ibid., 11.
7. Ibid., 177.
8. Ibid., 12.
9. Ibid., 14.
10. Ibid., 14–15.
11. Geisler and Nix, *A General Introduction to the Bible*, 267, 272.
12. Ibid., 269.
13. Ibid.
14. Ibid., 271, 275.
15. Ibid., 271.
16. Ibid.
17. Ibid., 272.
18. Frank Crane, *The Lost Books of the Bible* (New York: Bell, 1979).
19. See discussion in "Books That Almost Made It," *Christian History* 13, no. 3 [Issue 43, 1994], 30–31.

Reason Seven: The Bible Has Power to Change Lives

1. Kenneth S. Wuest, *Hebrews in the Greek New Testament* (Grand Rapids: Eerdmans, 1948), 89.
2. Ibid., 87.
3. Ibid., 88, 89.
4. Sam Harris, *Letter to a Christian Nation* (New York: Alfred A. Knopf, 2006), ix.
5. Douglas Wilson, *Letter from a Christian Citizen* (Powder Springs, GA: American Vision, 2007), 9.
6. Harris, *Letter to a Christian Nation*, 8.
7. Gary DeMar, http://74.255.56.30/blog/?p=53.
8. Christopher Hitchens and Douglas Wilson, "Is Christianity Good for the World?" (New York: Twelve, 2007), http://www.ChristianityToday.com/CT/2007/mayweb-only/119-12.0.html.
9. Richard Dawkins, *The God Delusion* (New York: Houghton Mifflin, 2006), 14.
10. Ibid., 57.
11. Alvin J. Schmidt, *How Christianity Changed the World*, formerly *Under the Influence* (Grand Rapids: Zondervan, 2004), 71.
12. Ibid., 79–80, 85.
13. Ibid., 248.
14. Arthur Brooks *Who Really Cares* (New York: Basic Books, 2006).
15. Harris, *Letter to a Christian Nation*, viii.
16. Charles Spurgeon, "The Word a Sword," in *The Treasury of the Bible: The New Testament*, vol. 4 (reprint; Grand Rapids: Zondervan, 1962), 40.

For Doubters Only

1. Stan Guthrie, "Answering the Atheists," *The Weekly Newsletter of Christianity Today International*, November 13, 2007.
2. C. S. Lewis, "Religion: Reality or Substitute?" in *Christian Reflections*, ed. Walter Hooper (Grand Rapids: Eerdmans, 1967), 42–43.
3. J. B. Phillips, *Ring of Truth* (London: Hodder & Stoughton, 1967), 47–48.

MORE BOOKS BY
ERWIN W. LUTZER

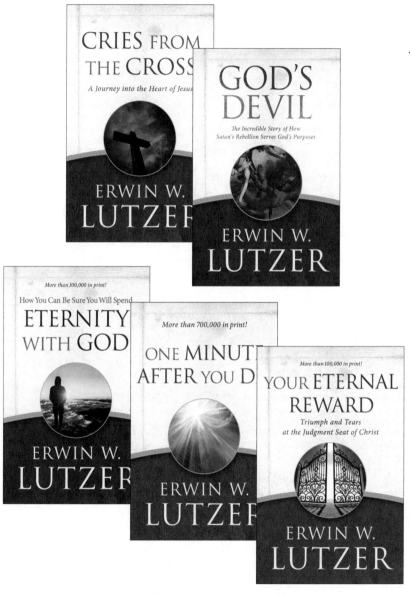

CRIES FROM THE CROSS
A Journey into the Heart of Jesus
ERWIN W. LUTZER

GOD'S DEVIL
The Incredible Story of How Satan's Rebellion Serves God's Purposes
ERWIN W. LUTZER

More than 100,000 in print!
How You Can Be Sure You Will Spend
ETERNITY WITH GOD
ERWIN W. LUTZER

More than 700,000 in print!
ONE MINUTE AFTER YOU DIE
ERWIN W. LUTZER

More than 100,000 in print!
YOUR ETERNAL REWARD
Triumph and Tears at the Judgment Seat of Christ
ERWIN W. LUTZER

MOODY Publishers™

From the Word to Life

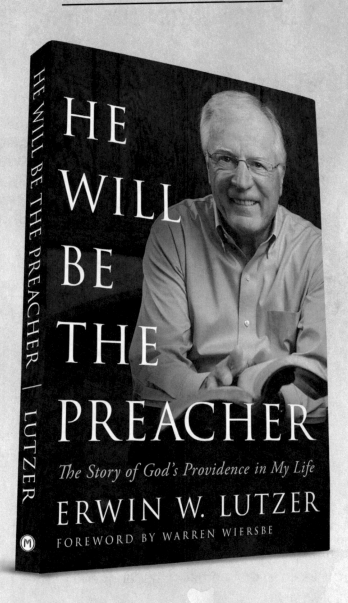

HE WILL BE THE PREACHER | LUTZER

HE WILL BE THE PREACHER

The Story of God's Providence in My Life

ERWIN W. LUTZER

FOREWORD BY WARREN WIERSBE

MOODY
Publishers™

From the Word to Life

MOODY
Radio™

*From the Word **to Life***

Moody Radio produces and delivers compelling programs filled with biblical insights and creative expressions of faith that help you take the next step in your relationship with Christ.

You can hear Moody Radio on 36 stations and more than 1,500 radio outlets across the U.S. and Canada. Or listen on your smartphone with the Moody Radio app!

www.moodyradio.org